A Ghost in My Suitcase

A Guide to Haunted Travel in America

by Mitchel Whitington

Atriad Press • Dallas, Texas

Inquiries should be addressed to

Atriad Press
13820 Methuen Green
Dallas Texas, 75240
972-671-0002

www.atriadpress.com

Library of Congress Control Number 2005903313

International Standard Book Number 0-9740394-5-4

The editors wish to thank Alan McCuller for the outstanding cover art, and Martha McCuller for the beautiful interior design. We are very grateful for their contributions.

Printed in the United States of America

For Tami, my incredible wife, who has not only tirelessly accompanied me to countless haunted locations around the country over the years, but also puts up with way too many hours with me in front of the computer writing about them. Thanks, babe — this book wouldn't have been possible without you.

And for Big Steve — the reason why is in the pages of this book.

Contents

Contents

Contents

A Ghost in My Suitcase

Ah, a ghost in my suitcase — what better way to see America? Actually, it's not your luggage that may have a spirit or two. Instead, it is the places that we'll be visiting on our haunted adventure around the country. Together we'll stop in every single state, from Maine to California, Washington to Florida, and everything in between.

These aren't tall tales around the campfire. We're going to be visiting some of the most haunted places in the United States, and exploring both the history and the tales of the ghosts that walk there today. It's going to be a lot of fun, and hopefully we'll get an occasional chill running down our spine! In the course of our journey, we'll visit the dark and dank Shanghai Tunnels in Portland, Oregon; delve into the mysterious past of the LaLaurie Mansion in New Orleans, Louisiana; check out the strange tales of The Grove in Jefferson, Texas; stop to hear about a young girl's tragic tale at Emily's Bridge in Stowe, Vermont; and make forty-six other spirited stopovers that you'll find simply fascinating.

At each location, we're going to look into the background of the place and the hauntings that continue to occur. Sometimes we'll rely on the stories from the people who live and work there, but at some places you'll find that supernatural activity actually occurred during the writing of this book. You never know what's going to happen at the next stop.

Hopefully you'll want to visit some of these locations on your own, so in preparation for that here are a few basic items to consider:

1) Understand what a haunted encounter really is. It isn't always a full-form apparition that you'll see floating down a hallway at midnight. Sometimes it's a strong smell of perfume or tobacco. On other occasions, you might experience a feeling of intense emotion. The list goes on and on — just keep your senses open, and be aware of everything around you.

2) Think quiet time, not nighttime. Most people think that ghostly activity happens at midnight, or some other time of evening. This usually is not the case. Instead, find times when there aren't as many people around, and therefore less distractions are present. When visiting a haunted hotel, I'd much rather go on a Monday or Tuesday night when it is less occupied. For restaurants with a spirited reputation, you'll find me there before or after the meal crowd. If I'm taking a walking tour, my first question when booking the reservation is, "When will it be least crowded?" Remove as many distractions as possible, and you're much more likely to have a brush with the supernatural.

3) Respect the location, the people who live or work there, and, certainly not least of all, the spirits that might frequent the place. Don't enter where you haven't been invited, be courteous and unobtrusive, and consider that in some places the folks there may not want to openly discuss their haunting. After all, not everyone welcomes the idea of ghosts — the very idea can sometimes be unnerving.

4) The majority of the places in this book are very safe, and are open to people who want to visit there. Do be aware, though, that you should always keep your safety in the back of your mind. Most any city will have some areas that are more dangerous than others, especially when the sun goes down. While we're all going to enter

the realm of the spirit world one of these days, I'd like us all to stay in this dimension as long as possible.

All that said, it's time to get started on our journey. On a personal note, I'm honored that you've chosen to accompany me on the trip. We're going to have a good time, and find a ghost or two along the way. So pack your bags, toss them in the car, and let's get going. Who knows? By the time we're done, you might even find a ghost in your suitcase...

The Foundry Phantoms

Sloss Furnace — Birmingham, Alabama

OUR FIRST STOP on this ghostly tour of America is Birmingham, Alabama. If you're like me, one of the first things that you'll notice is that up on Red Mountain, overlooking the city, is a massive statue of Vulcan. Not a science-fiction character with pointy ears, but instead the Roman god who was an architect, blacksmith, armorer, chariot builder, and artist. The fifty-six foot statue holds a hammer in his left hand and a spearhead in his right, proclaiming the god's particular prowess as a smith. The spearhead is fitted with a light that glows green if there have been no traffic fatalities in the last twenty-four hours, and red if a person has died in an accident in that time period. I have to tell you, he's impressive.

It is fitting that Vulcan should oversee the city, because it gained a reputation not all that long after it was incorporated in 1871 as one of the leading centers for iron production. A man named Colonel James Withers Sloss, a veteran of the Civil War, realized that a quality iron could be manufactured from the iron ore in the Birmingham area, using coke that would be manufactured from Alabama coal. He directed a company in 1876 that was

1

able to prove that this process worked, and so he founded the Sloss Furnace Company, which began producing iron in 1882. During that time, Birmingham began to experience a tremendous explosion in growth, earning it the nickname "The Magic City."

The colonel sold the business in 1887 to a group of investors. It went through several incarnations, but continued to produce a quality grade of iron that was shipped around the country. It was used in the cars manufactured in Michigan and in the framework of buildings across the United States.

By 1971, the company was owned by U.S. Pipe, which found that it was no longer profitable to operate. They extinguished the fires in the great furnaces and gave the plant to the city as a reminder of its past.

While the plant was open, it wasn't without its ghost stories. In fact, more than a few spirits are thought to still lurk there.

One of the suspected phantoms is the spirit of James Wormwood, a foreman of the graveyard shift that ran from late night to early morning. The main job of the employees on that shift was to keep the furnaces burning so that they would be ready when the workers arrived the next day.

The graveyard shift was a brutal one — stoking up the fires brought the temperatures in the workrooms over one hundred and twenty degrees. Most of these workers were immigrants who could get no other work, and without money to live on they had no choice but to stay in the overcrowded housing that was near the furnace. This meant that they could be called back to work at any time of day or night, and would often function on very little sleep.

To make matters worse, the foreman Wormwood would drive the employees in his charge to their very limits. There were no holidays, no vacations, and no rest for the weary ironworkers. Wormwood made them slave away long hours and take risks to increase production. Many workers were injured on his grave-yard shifts, including some who were maimed and could no longer work. Several were blinded in explosions, and forty-seven men lost their lives while working for the man that they nick-named "The Slag."

In October 1906, James "The Slag" Wormwood met a fate that many workers felt was very appropriate. He was patrolling the top of the largest blast furnace — "Big Alice" — and some-how stumbled. He tumbled into the vat of molten iron ore, where he was instantly vaporized.

Few workers grieved, and there were even whisperings that some of the disgruntled staff had reached their limit with him and tossed him into the vat. The official report said that he was over-come by the methane gas that was a by-product from the furnace and lost his balance, even though Wormwood usually didn't walk above the furnaces as part of his job.

The graveyard shift was shut down; the company's stated position was that the high number of accidents was detrimental to their overall operation.

The murmurings about Slag Wormwood didn't go away, though. Soon after his death, the workers at the plant began to report a strange feeling — an unearthly presence that they couldn't explain. Some believe that his brutality continued from beyond the grave. In 1926, for example, a night watchman was shoved from behind and heard a gruff voice say, "Get back to work!" When he looked around, though, he was alone — not a single living being was in the area.

Although the reports of strange occurrences continued on a regular basis, another major event happened twenty-one years later in 1947. Three supervisors could not be located at the plant, and a search of the premises was launched. They were finally found locked in a small boiler room, unconscious, and not a single one of them could explain what had happened. The only thing that they could remember was seeing a badly burned man who was yelling at them to get back to work and "push some steel!"

Slag was blamed for many things that happened at the plant through the years, but one item attributed to him was very tragic. In 1971, on the evening before the Sloss Furnaces were to close for good, a night watchman on a routine stroll through the plant encountered what he described as an evil being, burned and disfigured, half man and half demon. The creature pushed him, but the watchman held his ground. The assailant then pounded on the poor man with his fists until the watchman collapsed.

When he was examined by a doctor, the night watchman was found to be covered with severe burns. He never recovered from the injuries.

While the spirit of Slag Wormwood may walk the grounds of the plant, he is not alone. Another haunting there is attributed to a man named Theophilus Calvin Jowers. In 1887 he was named to the position of assistant foundryman on "Big Alice," the foundry that would eventually take Slag's life. He was walking around the edge of the furnace on a shift and lost his balance. He fell into the vat of iron and was immediately consumed by the heat. Workmen who tried to fish his body out of the molten liquid could only find a foot and shoe that hadn't been vaporized.

Jowers was seen at the foundry until it closed, especially around "Big Alice." He was never threatening, but always seemed intent on doing his job — walking around the furnace, checking the work that was being done, and just generally keeping an eye on things. Many people saw him, and knew that the figure must be a ghost; he was often walking closer to the heat than a human being could possibly withstand and still survive.

While those two ghosts have been recognized by workers, there is another spirit that is more of a legend. As the story goes, a young girl who lived in the early part of the 1900s found herself pregnant. She was overcome with worry and grief — being an unwed mother at that time brought shame to the entire family.

Some family members worked at Sloss, so she knew of the huge foundries and the molten iron that they contained. Legend has it that she climbed up the walkways to the top of one and threw herself in. Soon, people began seeing a young doe at the plant, especially during ceremonies when many people were there. Some people believe that it is the spirit of the girl returning in a form of innocence. Sightings of the deer have been documented in print on several occasions.

Once the plant closed and was reopened as a museum honoring the steel and iron industry of Birmingham, the hauntings didn't stop. Many visitors today report seeing a shadowy figure walking by or hearing one of the plant's steam whistles blow at an odd time when no human is causing it to do so. Occasionally, someone is touched by an unseen hand as they tour the facility.

That doesn't seem to stop the crowds, though, because Sloss Furnaces is a popular place to visit. Not only is it a National Historic Landmark, but there are tours and special programs to acquaint guests with the process of iron manufacturing. You'll find other special events such as a music festival, a kudzu festival, a birthday celebration for the plant, and, during the Halloween season, even a "haunted house" there. The latter is probably the most interesting. After all, when is the last time that you've been to a "haunted house" attraction that features *actual* ghosts?

Sloss Furnaces National Historic Landmark
Twenty 32nd Street North
Birmingham, AL 35222
(205) 324-1911
www.slossfurnaces.com

Ghosts of the Gold Rush

▬▬▬ ◦ ● ● ● ◦ ▬▬▬

The Golden North Hotel — Skagway, Alaska

PEOPLE SOMETIMES QUESTION why one building happens to be haunted while another is not. One of the best places to start to answer such a question is to look back into a location's history — it often can hold many answers. Such is the case with the Golden North Hotel in Skagway, Alaska. There are several phantoms that roam its hallways, but to understand why, let's take a look at the story behind the city itself.

Skagway is truly a town founded on the legendary "gold rush fever" that was responsible for settling so much of the wilderness country in the United States.

Alaska is one of those unbelievable land deals that happened in North America over the years: The Dutch purchased Manhattan Island from the Canarsee Delaware Indians for some finely crafted beads, the U.S. got the Louisiana Purchase for fifteen million dollars from France, and Alaska was purchased from Russia for the bargain price of seven million bucks. Now, that's certainly a lot of money, but not for all that oil-ridden acreage!

The popular theory is that Alaska was first populated by people who walked from Asia thousands of years ago across a land bridge traversing the Bering Strait. When the purchase was made by a treaty between the United States and Russia in 1867, Americans began to flock to this undiscovered country.

One such man was a steamboat captain named William Moore who lived nearby in Canada's Yukon Territory, who believed that a gold strike would occur in the mountains of the Klondike. He based his theory on the fact that the precious metal had been discovered in similar mountain ranges in British Columbia, South America, and North America. William also knew that throngs of prospectors would come from the contiguous United States to the south, and they would only have a few passages from which to choose. Knowing that many of them would be coming through the White Pass Trail at the mouth of the Skagway River in Alaska, he established a town there to handle the influx that he knew would soon began. With the help of his son, he constructed a log cabin as a home, a wharf for ships to dock with their passengers, and a sawmill to produce the lumber that would certainly accompany the boom.

It came in 1896 when three prospectors discovered gold in Rabbit Creek in Canada's Yukon Territory — specifically, in the outer reaches of the Klondike region. When the Klondike gold reached Seattle, Washington, aboard the S.S. *Portland*, thousands of people flocked northward to seek their fortunes. As William Moore predicted, many came up the inside water passage to take the White Pass Trail that started on Moore's land. Something interesting happened, however — the population boom came so fast that Moore was soon lost in the shuffle. A self-appointed city government began dividing up the land without regard to his initial claims, and Skagway, Alaska, was born. It was unable to handle the in-pouring of prospectors, so much of the town became a tent city. The living conditions were primitive at best; waste from the mules and houses filled the streets, and with no police or military presence, crime was rampant.

Travel conditions on White Pass Trail worsened by 1897, and it became almost impassable. Only ten percent of those who set out for it made it through — it was a challenge for humans, but almost impossible for supply-laden horses and mules. The rest returned to Skagway, often leaving the carcasses of their pack animals along the trail. It became such a disgusting place that White Pass soon became known as "Dead Horse Trail."

People continued to arrive, however, and with the money that they spent there, the town began to transform from a rough settlement to something a little more like a well-planned city. In 1898, the Klondike Trading Company, one of those investing in Skagway, constructed a large building for its offices.

Skagway had its ups and downs in the next few years: In 1897 its population was seven hundred, but that grew to twenty thousand by 1898. By 1899, however, the population was back at seven hundred people. It would stay there for years to come, and in fact is just about that number today.

In 1908, the Klondike Trading Company did not need its office building any more, and it was opened as the Golden North Hotel, a plush stopover for those who still had their sight set on a fortune in gold, or those merchants hoping to make their wealth in the city.

The hotel played host to countless people over the years, but one of the most famous stories of a guest there comes from the gold rush days. A young couple came to town to get married and raise enough money by striking gold to set them up for the rest of their lives. The young lady checked into the Golden North Hotel, and her fiancé went off toward the gold fields to find their fortune.

Because of the ruffians and robbers who roamed the streets of Skagway, the girl was terrified to leave the Golden North. She spent her days wandering the hallways of the hotel and looking out of the window in hopes of catching a glimpse of her fiancé.

She hoped that he would be returning to her laden with gold to pave the way for their future.

In the course of the wait, the young girl fell ill with pneumonia, and her condition spiraled swiftly downward. Her life slipped away as she lay there alone in the bed of Room 23. When her young man finally did return, he found that his love had been long-buried. The young man was grief-stricken, and left the city burdened with sorrow instead of gold.

It seems that the girl did not permanently leave the hotel, however. It wasn't long until guests and staff at the Golden North began to see the ghostly figure of a girl — the one who had died of pneumonia — continuing to walk the halls. She was seen so often by the staff, in fact, that they gave her a name: Mary.

Mary understandably seems to favor Room 23. For some reason, she also seems to frequent Room 14, because guests there have seen a lighted form moving around the room during their stay.

In the hallway, employees of the hotel have heard light footsteps walking along; when they turn around, expecting to see a guest passing by, the hallway is empty. If you take a moment to talk to the hotel staff, you will quickly discover that there is hardly a person who doesn't have a ghost story to tell.

Many mysterious things happen at the Golden North Hotel. In Room 23, however, the sightings are much more definitive. The spectral form of a young girl has been spotted standing beside the bed, and has even shown up in photographs taken by guests. Chambermaids have reported the presence of Mary numerous times, and on one occasion the hotel manager accompanied a maid to investigate one of the sightings. When the manager opened the door to Room 23, they encountered Mary in one of the most dramatic sightings to date. As they entered, they saw the lone form of a female standing by the window, looking out across the city, as if she were watching for her fiancé to come walking down the street of Skagway to claim her. The spirit turned around, bowed her head, and slowly faded away, perhaps knowing that she would never again see her fiancé.

Skagway, Alaska, is a beautiful town with a backdrop of snow-capped mountains and a wonderfully historic place to visit. Be sure to book your room at the Golden North Hotel — in Room 23, if you dare. While no harm will come to you there, it is possible that you will encounter the spirit of a very lonely girl, hoping to see her fiancé one last time.

The Golden North Hotel
3rd and Broadway Streets
P.O. Box 343
Skagway, AK 99840
www.goldennorthhotel.com

Only a Bird in a Gilded Cage

The Bird Cage Theatre — Tombstone, Arizona

TO GET READY for this leg of our journey, I'd first recommend renting the movie *Tombstone* starring Kurt Russell as the legendary gunfighting sheriff Wyatt Earp. Walking down historic Allen Street, I defy anyone to keep the film's images from popping into their head. It is so easy to look around and imagine the places from all over town as they were in those bawdy old days: the Grand Hotel, Boot Hill, the O.K. Corral, and, of course, the Bird Cage Theatre.

In the movie, the Bird Cage is portrayed as a place for a traveling vaudeville show to entertain the locals, and the Earp brothers are shown sitting up in the "bird cages" with their wives as if they were theater boxes in a fancy establishment. Truth be known, no respectable lady would even walk on the street in front of the Bird Cage Theatre — much less set foot inside.

In reality, these theater-type boxes were individual rooms where the ladies of the evening who worked the theater could entertain their clients. It was possible to open the curtains in each box so that the ladies and their gentlemen friends could

11

drink and watch the goings-on below on the floor, or the drapes could be pulled for a more intimate rendezvous.

In 1881, the famous Broadway writer/composer Arthur J. Lamb was visiting the Bird Cage Theatre with Eddy Foy, a great performer of the time. The business had just opened, and William Hutchinson — the owner of the establishment — had dubbed his theater and gaming house The Elite. It was the first visit to The Elite for both men, and they were studying the beautiful, plush interior of the theater. "It reminds me of a coffin," Foy remarked, "long and narrow."

Lamb just laughed and pointed up at the balconies trimmed in gold. "See those girls in the scanty costumes with the colored feathers in their hair? Well, they remind me of birds in little gilded cages hanging up there." After studying them a bit more, he said, "And like birds in cages, they probably don't have a chance in the world of making it out of this place."

Foy shrugged and said, "Sounds like you've got a good song there."

Lamb realized that his friend was right, and immediately started scratching the words down on a napkin from the bar. Later in the day, Lamb sat at the theater's grand piano, picking out a tune on the keys to accompany the words. Foy listened to the first rendition of the song, and reportedly told Lamb, "That's one hell of a good song, but not one for me. It's a song that only a lady should sing."

After working on the song for a bit longer, Lamb presented "She's Only a Bird in a Gilded Cage" to a then-unknown female singer booked at The Elite. She performed it that same night to a standing ovation and eight encores. Her name was Lillian Russel, and she became one of the stars of song and stage of the period. Lamb's song became a benchmark of nineteenth century music and the theme for the establishment. That first night after it was sung there, Hutchinson immediately changed the name of the place from The Elite to The Bird Cage Theatre.

One of the things that you'll learn when visiting the Bird Cage is that not only was it a theater, but it was also the home to many a game of chance. Doc Holliday was known to deal faro there occasionally, and it was on one such night when the famous "handkerchief duel" took place. Doc was drinking steadily as he dealt, like he often did, and was well on his way to inebriation when Johnny Ringo strolled in. Johnny was a known killer and member of the notorious "Cowboy Gang," and had been imbibing quite a bit himself on that evening.

When their paths crossed, Doc took a drink and taunted Johnny from behind the gambling table. "Care to buck the tiger? It's the gutsiest game in town." "Bucking the tiger" was another term for faro, so in essence Doc was daring Johnny Ringo to play a hand against him.

Ringo stopped, pulled off the signature red scarf that the Cowboy Gang wore, and waved it at him. "Care to grab the other end of this bandanna, Doc? It's the *deadliest* game in town."

Johnny was challenging Doc to one of the most fatal duels of the Old West, where each man took an end of a handkerchief, then drew their guns with the other. Because of the point-blank nature of the fight, both participants were almost always wounded, and often killed.

Doc smiled, staring at his adversary, and reportedly said, "I'm your huckleberry, Johnny — this may just be my lucky day." With that, he grabbed the dangling end of the red handkerchief and pulled his gun. Ringo pulled his at the same time, and in the split second before both men fired, an associate of Johnny's named Curly Bill Brocius slapped the killer's gun away, yelling, "Hell, Doc, he's drunk!"

Both men fired, and both missed — Ringo because his gun had been deflected away and Doc because he was so intoxicated.

When Holliday saw this, he laughed and told Bill, "Well, I drink more by ten in the morning than he does all day." With that, he strolled away, ending Tombstone's famous handkerchief duel.

When you visit the Bird Cage, you'll see many bullet holes in the walls that have been left there over the years as a reminder of its colorful past. The stories aren't limited to the six-guns of the West, however. One of the most famous tales concerns a working girl named Margarita. While the music was playing one evening and the ladies were entertaining their clients in the draped boxes upstairs, she was flirting with a high-stakes gambler named Billy Milgreen, sitting on his lap and lavishing him with attention. The girls at the Bird Cage were very territorial, so when Billy's "regular girl" came in, a lady known as "Gold Dollar," she was incensed at Margarita taking her client away so publicly. She pulled a stiletto knife and stabbed Margarita in the chest. It was such a vicious crime that some say she intended to cut the girl's heart out, and stopped only when she heard warnings that the sheriff had been called. She ran out of the back door of the theater, perhaps the one that visitors today walk through into the gift shop, and disappeared into the night. No charges were ever filed against her, because there was no murderess and no murder weapon. Oddly enough, a little over a hundred years later the stiletto was unearthed behind the building. It is now on display at the Bird Cage, a twenty-first century memorial to Margarita.

The theater today isn't an operating bar for tourists, but has instead been converted into a museum. You can walk along the floor in the footsteps of the Earp brothers and their friend Doc Holliday, and see literally thousands of items that are on display, from Bird Cage memorabilia to Tombstone city artifacts. Some folks might find it all a little kitsch, and in a few cases I'd be inclined to agree — witness the mummified remains of a mermaid, for example. But all in all, the Bird Cage Theatre is just plain fun. I stood there on the stage where performers such as

Eddy Foy, Lillian Russel, Lotta Crabtree, Lily Langtree, and Lola Montez had entertained the rough trade of Tombstone, and just soaked in all of the ambiance of the place. It was magnificent.

With all the rich history of the Bird Cage, it's easy to understand how it got such a haunted reputation. Ghost hunters from around the country flock to the theater to take photographs and look for cold spots and other anomalies that signal the presence of an otherworldly visitor.

If scenes of violence or other intense emotion seems to be a focus for the presence of ghosts, then this theater would be a perfect place to find them. In 1882, *The New York Times* named the Bird Cage Theatre "the roughest, bawdiest, and most wicked night spot between Basin Street and the Barbary Coast." During the time that it operated — nine years — the doors were never closed and the party went on 24/7. It was the site of the world's longest-running poker game, and the scene of twenty-six deaths from sixteen gun and knife fights. Between one hundred and two hundred bullet holes pockmark the walls, floors, and ceilings of the building. But with all that violence, one shouldn't forget the girls. The "gilded cages" were places of passion, and customers ranged from local businessmen stepping out on their wives to cowboys blowing through town seeking their fortunes. More raw emotion of every kind was probably vented here than any other place in Arizona.

So what spirits haunt the Bird Cage? Quite a few, apparently. Most ghost hunters return from a visit there with photos of inexplicable orbs of light in the main theater, on the stage, and even in the backstage area. The folks who work there tell stories of many guests over the years who have asked questions about things that they simply can't explain. Visitors will ask about the voices coming from the birdcage boxes, when there isn't a single person up there. People standing outside of the theater hear singing, sometimes accompanied by the tinkling of a piano, but when the sound is investigated the huge room is completely empty but for the silent pieces of the museum. Tourists and employees through the years have reported seeing people in clothing from the boomtown days of Tombstone. Initially mistaken for the many period actors in town, they disappear suddenly or fade away into the shadows. The one specter who has been reported with some regularity is a man in a visor who lingers on the stage.

The city of Tombstone itself is rife with visitors from the spirit world, and there are stories from many places in the town, including the old Boot Hill cemetery and Big Nose Kate's Saloon, which was originally the Grand Hotel. Perhaps none are as haunted, though, as the Bird Cage Theatre.

I enjoyed our stay in town, visited all of those places, and even watched the gunfight reenactment right there in the street. Of all the memories that I took from Tombstone, though, I think that I'll most remember standing on the stage of the Bird Cage, looking out across the theater, then closing my eyes and letting my mind wander back to those days of Wyatt, Doc, and the Clanton brothers.

Buck the tiger, Doc? Why sure, deal me in.

The Bird Cage Theatre
517 East Allen St.
Tombstone, AZ 85638
(520) 457-3421

The Spirit of Michael

The Crescent Hotel — Eureka Springs, Arkansas

IF ANY PLACE could conceivably be haunted, it is the Crescent Hotel in Eureka Springs. The "Grand Old Lady of the Ozarks" was built in 1886 as a resort for those seeking the healing waters that flow from beneath the mountains in the area. It was constructed by Irish stonemasons from Chicago who did a masterful job — the hotel resembles a stately mansion that overlooks the city below. During construction, a worker fell from the upper scaffolding down onto the second floor slab, where he died in the area that is now Room 218. There were a few other injuries but no more deaths, and the hotel was completed on schedule. The regal front doors opened into the lobby where guests were greeted with every amenity imaginable. For twenty years, people flocked to the hotel to breathe the fresh mountain air and immerse themselves in mineral baths. The popularity of healing waters waned, however, and the Crescent fell on hard times. Just after the turn of the century, the front doors to the elegant lobby closed.

In 1908, a group of investors purchased the building and opened it as the Crescent College and Conservatory for Young

Women. The accommodations were first class, the faculty was prestigious, and wealthy families from across the nation sent their daughters to the exclusive Eureka Springs school. One semester took a tragic turn when a student fell in love with a local boy from a poor family in town. Her father forbade her to continue the relationship, and in desperation, the girl reportedly threw herself from the uppermost balcony of the building. The incident was hushed up, and enrollments continued. Even with the high price of tuition, however, the school was not financially viable for its investors, and the doors closed again in 1924.

Several businesses tried to make a go at the Crescent over the next few years, until in 1937 it was purchased by Doctor Norman Baker to be used as a health resort. Baker had to tiptoe around the law because his title of doctor was self-conferred, and he had recently been in trouble in Iowa for practicing medicine without a license. He brought his guaranteed "six-week cure for cancer" to the Crescent, however, and replaced the stately decor of the hotel with bright art-deco designs featuring his signature color: purple. Some people hold that Baker was a harmless man who hoped to heal the terminally ill with the local mineral water. Others tell stories of horrible experiments that he conducted on patients to try to discover the ultimate cure for cancer, with footnotes of midnight cremations and cancerous limbs in jars sealed in the walls of the basement. Whatever the truth may be, many people died in the hotel over the Baker years — the "doctor" was simply unable to make good on his guarantee of healing. The American Medical Association alerted the authorities about his new hospital, and Norman Baker was convicted in 1940 and sentenced to serve four years in Leavenworth. Yet again, the doors to the building were locked, and the Grand Old Lady sat silent on the hillside.

In 1946, the building was purchased once again, this time with the intent of restoring the hotel to its original glamour. To put it simply, the new owners succeeded. Today it is a magnificent place full of history and more than a few ghost stories.

My wife and I knew most of this going in, so we called far enough in advance to have our pick of the rooms. As always, we started out by asking where most of the paranormal activity had been taking place recently. The desk clerk just laughed, as if she got that question every day, and said, "More things happen in Michael's room than anywhere else in the hotel." That was all we needed to hear; one minute later we had reservations for three nights in Room 218.

Ghosts or not, when we arrived we were very pleased with the hotel. It was architecturally impressive, and the staff was looking after us from the moment we stepped inside. After checking in, the bell captain took our luggage and led us to Room 218.

We couldn't help but ask, "Any supernatural stories from the room lately?"

He smiled, shrugged his shoulders, and said, "Well, if you do find a ghost in the Crescent, it will probably be in here." With that he laid down our bags, gave us a little info about the hotel, and left us alone in the room. We hadn't unpacked the first suitcase when the door to the room began to rattle, and we heard a few muffled thumps from the hallway. My wife was standing next to the door, so she slowly turned the knob and pulled the door open, not knowing what to expect. As the light from our room spilled out into the dim hallway, two teenaged girls screamed, just about the time their father snapped their photo in front of the now-open door to notorious Room 218. They'd apparently heard the stories as well, and were getting a souvenir picture taken when we managed to scare the bejesus out of them.

"Have you seen anything?" they asked in unison.

My wife shook her head. "We just got here. Hopefully we will, though." That bit of excitement out of the way, we finished unpacking just in time to grab a bite at the elegant Crystal Dining Room before the hotel's ghost walk began. Even though our attire was shorts and tee shirts, we were treated like royalty — and the food was delicious.

The ghost walk was fifteen dollars per person, so we laid our thirty bucks on the table and each received an orange dot for our shirt to indicate that we had paid for the tour. After several more people signed up, we were on our way. The walk was led by two paranormal investigators who had been researching the hotel for quite some time. The first stop? Room 218 — Michael's Room — our room! We then received the worst news of the trip. It seems that Michael, the worker who fell to his death during the construction of the hotel, likes to play with people who don't really believe in the paranormal. He has appeared in his dusty overalls and work-shirt at the foot of the bed, touched people on the shoulder, called their name, and even reached out of the mirror to a man who was shaving one evening — but Michael rarely makes himself known to people who are actually looking for him. We looked at each other, sighed, and decided that it was just our luck to share quarters with such a spirit.

There are many other ghosts in the hotel, so our hopes were still high. A young lady dressed in an old-fashioned white dress has been seen wandering the garden, only to slowly vanish when someone addresses her. Many believe this to be the spirit of the girl who took her own life during the college days of the hotel. Another apparition, that of a man in a dark suit, sits in the old bar area off of the lobby, as if nursing a drink in silence. When people try to strike up a conversation with him, he seems to be listening intently, until he disappears when they happen to glance away.

Several rooms other than 218 have also been the sites of ghostly activity. In Room 203, an invisible presence stretched out on the bed beside a woman staying there. A guest snapping a photo in Room 202 caught the image of a ghostly person in the picture. People have reported a strange feeling in Room 305, like some unseen person was in the room with them. Phantom nurses have been seen pushing gurneys down the second and third floor hallways, as if some scene from the past was being replayed over and over. The Crescent is full of stories like this and many, many more. What you may be wondering at this point, however, is: *What did we experience there?*

When the ghost walk had ended, we grabbed a couple of drinks from the bar to take onto our room's massive outside porch. My wife sipped a glass of wine, I had an ice-cold pilsner, and we just sat there reading and occasionally staring at the beautiful view of the valley before us. When it became too dark to read, we went back inside, and I said, "Well, Michael, I understand that you won't be paying us a visit tonight because we'd like so much to see you." I raised the last swallow in my glass. "That's too bad, because as an Irishman, I thought that you might be pleased if I left you a little beer!" Nothing happened, nor did I expect it to, so I downed that swallow and we both lay down on the bed to continue reading the books that we'd started. Suddenly, there were three distinct, rhythmic pops from the headboard. We sat up, looked at each other, and I know that we were both thinking, "Michael?" I tried duplicating the sound by knocking on the headboard, but couldn't even come close. We decided that it sounded like the popping that wood makes when it is under pressure, just before it breaks. At that point, the fact that Michael had fallen from the scaffolding several floors up and crashed through to the concrete second floor wasn't lost on us.

We eventually turned in for the night, and about four in the morning were awakened by the same sound, this time ten to twelve methodical pops from the headboard. We tried every rational explanation that we could conjure to explain the sounds but simply couldn't. The second night, the sounds issued from the headboard once again. On the third and final night that we were there, the two of us were laying in bed reading again, when my wife looked up from her book suddenly. "Someone's in here," she told me. I asked how she knew, but she just shook her head and went on to explain that it was just the kind of feeling that you get when you're not alone. Nodding over toward the far corner of the room, by the door, she got up and walked slowly in that direction; of course, I followed. When we got there, the air was something that I can only describe as "heavy," as if you had to push yourself into it a little. The hairs on our arms stood up, and there was definitely the sensation of being in the presence of a third person. In only a moment, it was gone, as if the person had walked through the door and out of the room. We had no indication of who it might have been, but in my mind, I have to believe that it was Michael just saying goodbye, especially since he'd been giving us a few audible indications of his presence on the previous two nights.

If we ever return to the Crescent Hotel, and I'm sure that we will, I'm going to ask for Room 218 again. This time, I'm bringing along a few bottles of Guinness — something that no good Irishman, dead or alive, could resist.

The Crescent Hotel
75 Prospect Ave.
Eureka Springs, AR 72632
(800) 342-9766
http://www.crescent-hotel.com
http://www.eureka-springs-ghost.com

The Obsession of Sarah Winchester

The Winchester Mystery House — San Jose, California

THERE ARE MANY legends about the spirits inhabiting the old Winchester Mansion in San Jose, California. Since it is a tourist attraction today, I wondered whether the stories were true accounts or simply tales for the sightseers. With my first visit to the mansion — now called the "Winchester Mystery House" — any such questions were put aside.

To start to understand whatever supernatural activity might be going on there, you first have to examine the history of the house. In September 1862 Sarah married William Wirt Winchester, who was the sole heir to the Winchester Repeating Rifle fortune created by the sale of the famed "rifle that won the West." They were the toast of proper society in New Haven, Connecticut, and in July of 1866, the couple had a daughter that they named Annie. Six months later, disease took Annie's life, and Sarah never recovered from the tragedy. William developed tuberculosis and died in March 1881, leaving Sarah completely alone. She was totally devastated, and her friends began to worry about her mental and physical health.

Sarah was well taken care of by her husband's estate, however. She inherited twenty million dollars and a large portion of the Winchester Repeating Arms Company, from which she earned one thousand dollars a day in royalties. Unfortunately, the money didn't help — the widow was falling into a deep depression. A friend suggested that Sarah consult with a medium who might be able to console her by contacting the spirits of William and Annie. The spiritualist was not able to do that, but instead told Sarah that the lives of her husband and daughter had been taken due to a curse that had befallen the family. The perpetrators of the curse were the spirits of all the people who had been killed by the Winchester rifles. It was further explained to Sarah that the only way to appease these hostile spirits would be to purchase a home where they could reside, and continually add on to the house to accommodate the rising number of spirits killed by the rifles. The medium told her that should construction ever stop on the house, Sarah would die.

The widow Winchester immediately set out to find a suitable house. Because her husband died of tuberculosis, she wanted a climate with fresh, moist air — many people of the day thought that would prevent the disease. She settled on a house in San Jose, California, and began hiring carpenters as soon as she moved in. The sound of hammers and saws reverberated through the house twenty-four hours a day, seven days a week, three hundred sixty-five days a year. Sarah personally oversaw the construction, getting direction from the spirit world during nightly séances held in her special séance room.

The instructions that the spirits provided were often confusing to the workmen, but they followed her directions precisely. The mansion therefore contains staircases that lead only to the ceiling, doors that open to solid walls, a cabinet with shelves that are only half an inch deep, windows set into the floor, a door that opens to an eight-foot drop into the kitchen below, and a chimney that rises through four stories of the house only to stop suddenly a foot and a half from the roof. Some speculate that Sarah was trying to trick the spirits with the confusing layout of the house, while other people simply think that she was losing her mind. In any case, the structure is an architectural marvel today and is registered as a California Historical Landmark. It is open daily for tours, although time permits visitors to see only a fraction of the forty staircases, forty bedrooms, forty-seven fireplaces, seventeen chimneys, fifty-two skylights, almost two thousand doors, and approximately ten thousand windows. Still, it's a sight to behold.

The house is full of architectural oddities, including an overabundance of the number thirteen, which Sarah regarded as a "good" number. Her fascination with it is displayed throughout the house: windows with thirteen panes, chandeliers with thirteen lights, thirteen drain holes in the Italian kitchen sink, thirteen palm trees on the front drive, many stairways with thirteen steps, thirteen bathrooms — the thirteenth of which has thirteen windows, and thirteen hooks in the séance room for the thirteen robes that she wore while contacting the spirit world.

Another practice of the widow Winchester was to sleep in a different room every night. She could have been simply trying to make the most out of her massive home, but it was said that she did this to confuse the spirits. By constantly changing rooms, they would never know where to find her at night.

Every evening at midnight, Sarah would make her way up to her specially designed séance room, which had only one entrance but three exits. There she would wait for the large bell in the tower to be rung to summon the spirits who would give her instructions on how to proceed with construction on the house. Sometimes these sessions lasted for hours, and she was very secretive about them. At the end of the séance, somewhere around two in the morning, the bell was rung once again to signal the departure of the spirits.

On September 4, 1922, with her meeting with the spirits concluded, she made her way to a bedroom for a good night's sleep. Sometime during the early morning hours, Sarah died peacefully in her sleep at the ripe old age of some eighty-odd years. For the first time since she purchased the house, it fell silent. Legend has it that the workmen stopped abruptly, even leaving nails driven halfway into wood. Sarah's body was interred beside her husband and daughter, and the business of wrapping up the Winchester legacy began. When the will was read, it was found that it had — of course — thirteen parts and was signed thirteen times. It was found that Sarah's safe contained only two locks of hair, that of her husband and daughter, along with copies of their newspaper obituaries. No arrangements had been made for the mansion, and so it was sold, dubbed the "Winchester Mystery House," and opened to the public for tours.

The house is on Winchester Boulevard, just north of Interstate 280 and south of Stevens Creek Boulevard, and we found it without too much trouble. Like any good tourist attraction, you enter and leave through the souvenir shop, but that won't diminish the experience — trust me, you'll be too excited about getting to walk through Sarah's winding hallways.

When the tour begins, you are guided into the mansion to start an hour-long journey through the Winchester Mystery House. It is more fascinating than you can possibly imagine; the unique architecture has surprises around every corner.

The place is an architectural marvel, but it does have its share of eccentricities. Since Sarah was so small in stature, many of the stair steps are only a few inches high. Some entryways are downright tiny, and the layout of the house seems to have no rhyme or reason. I don't think that I'd be afraid to be lost in there alone, but I don't think that finding my way out would be a quick proposition.

Talking with some of the tour guides there, I learned several things — the first is that many of the staff members have ghost stories about the old place, but not all of them are willing to share — some keep the supernatural events to themselves. On the tour that I was on, though, the guide was more than willing to share. In fact, she said that when the house was being locked up one evening, she was in the carriage house portion where Mrs. Winchester's horse and buggy would pick her up and drop her off. She was making sure that no one was left inside, when a tall man in an old-fashioned black suit stepped quickly through. She ran after him, only to see him turn a corner and disappear in an empty hallway.

There are many ghostly stories about the house, including the sound of slamming doors in empty hallways and windows that open or close so violently that the glass inside shatters.

Visitors encounter cold spots as they walk through on tours, and ghostly balls of light have been captured on film, as well as being seen by the naked eye.

One occurrence that baffles the workers is the pealing of Sarah's spirit bell. The bell rings during the day when no one is near it, and has been heard in the early morning hours when the grounds are deserted and locked up tight.

Sounds seem to be one of the most frequent phenomena, whether it is organ music drifting through the rooms, footsteps echoing in the hallways, or the pounding of hammers from long ago drifting through the evening air.

No one knows whether or not the spirits of those killed by the repeating rifle haunt the house, but obviously some spirits still linger at the house that Sarah Winchester built.

Winchester Mystery House
525 South Winchester Blvd.
San Jose, CA 95128
(408) 247-2000
www.winchestermysteryhouse.com

The House That F.O. Built

— • ◦ ◉ ◦ • —

The Stanley Hotel — Estes Park, Colorado

THIS PARTICULAR CHAPTER was one of my favorites to write. To understand why, I'll tell you a quick story that has nothing to do with ghosts.

In 1979, my wife and I were living in a modest house on a wooded lot in the city of Hooks, Texas. On a shopping trip into Texarkana, we stopped by a bookstore and I found a paperback whose cover intrigued me. It was silver, and showed a line drawing of a boy's face with no features. It fascinated me, so I bought it and started reading. Later that evening, our basset hound, Fred, asked to go outside for a walk. I put his leash on him and we started out into the darkness.

The more Fred walked around sniffing for just the right tree, the more I thought back to the book that I'd been reading. It was a horror novel, and I had barely been able to put it down. I'd stopped at a scene where a fire hose was slithering after a little boy in the hallway of an isolated resort hotel, and quite frankly, I was terrified out there in the dark. I suddenly realized that the author had invoked this feeling in me. He was intentionally frightening me! I then knew that I wanted to have that power —

to evoke emotion in others. The book was *The Shining*, and the author was Stephen King.

Now, I don't write horror, but I do write about true spirits and hauntings. I enjoy giving people a shiver every now and then, and hopefully a smile or two as well. If I'd never picked up Mr. King's book, I might never have started down this path some twenty-odd years ago.

I saw the movie of *The Shining* that was done by Stanley Kubrick, and while it was a very entertaining show, it had many differences from the book. When the ABC miniseries was released, I like it quite a bit better. It was more faithful to the original story, and I also loved the hotel that was used as the backdrop. Where Kubrick had used mostly sets, the hotel used in the miniseries seemed to have a personality of its own.

It should — it was the very place that inspired King's wonderful book. In fact, he spent some time there in Room 217 while working on the story.

Every inch of the Stanley Hotel makes me think of *The Shining*, and makes me stop and contemplate applying for the job of babysitting the hotel through the winter, just to get to spend some time there completely alone — if you can ever be truly alone at the Stanley. Like the one in the story, the real hotel has its own set of otherworldly visitors. Unlike King's tale, though, these spirits are benevolent, not evil. Visitors flock there not only for the plush accommodations and pampering by the staff, but also in hopes of encountering one of the Stanley Hotel's resident ghosts.

Construction started on the hotel in 1907, and the doors officially opened in 1909. With almost a century's worth of guests coming and going at this luxurious resort, it's no wonder that a few of them have decided to come back for a while after death.

The hotel was the brainchild of Freelan Oscar Stanley — F.O. to his friends. He was an extremely successful businessman, gaining his wealth from the Stanley Dry Plate Company that he sold to a man named Kodak. He was also the inventor of the Stanley Steamer, a steam-powered automobile. In 1903, F.O.'s health began to deteriorate. When he went to his doctor, he weighed only one hundred eighteen pounds. The prognosis was bad: tuberculosis.

The doctor prescribed the fresh, cool mountain air of Colorado, so F.O. and his wife Flora packed up and moved to the Estes Park area. Having the entrepreneurial spirit that he did, F.O. was not content to simply sit and wait out his illness. Instead, he conceived a luxury hotel in the mountains and spent several years putting his plan into action. Since the city of Estes Park was still very rugged, he had to begin by creating an infrastructure that would support the hotel. He helped with the planning and building of a power plant, a water and waste disposal system, road improvements, and even basic businesses such as a medical facility, a financial institution, and more. A hydroelectric plant was constructed in the mountains so the hotel could be all-electric. To underscore the opulence of the place, a telephone was installed in every room — something that was unheard of at that time.

By 1909 the hotel was playing host to the first visitors, and it was already earning a reputation as a popular vacation destination. F.O. made use of his Stanley Steamer invention, engineering a bus dubbed the "Mountain Wagon" that could ferry passengers from railroad depots all over the region to his new hotel. Even though F.O. Stanley had been relegated to the mountains of Colorado for poor health, he turned the bad fortune into a magnificent business.

When you visit the Stanley Hotel today, you'll get to experience the hotel much as it was in F.O.'s day. There are very few major differences; one is the addition of heat to the hotel. When it was first opened, it was a summer resort and no heat was needed.

Now every room enjoys a climate-controlled environment. Other than that, things are pretty much the same — with the addition of a ghost or two, that is.

Who are these ghosts? Well, there haven't been any publicly recorded deaths at the hotel, so it's very likely that these are the spirits of people who, in life, visited the Stanley and remembered such a wonderful time there that they've chosen to return for an occasional afterlife visit.

The staff has many stories, and in fact it's difficult to find someone who's worked there any length of time who doesn't have a story about a haunted encounter. While the experiences vary, everyone agrees on one thing: The spirits of F.O. and Flora do occasionally return to visit the hotel that they built.

F.O. is most frequently seen in the billiard room, which was one of his favorite haunts when he was alive. Quite often he would simply hang out there, picking up a casual game with visitors to his hotel. It was something indeed to be offered a friendly game of billiards by a stranger during your visit, only to find out that you were shooting pool with the man who owned the place. F.O. was a master of customer relations — or perhaps he simply enjoyed a good game.

Since he loved it so much in life, he apparently comes back there now — he has been seen standing behind the billiards table, and even has intermingled with people walking through on a tour.

Flora, on the other hand, spends time in her own favorite room: the music room. To this day, it is home to a grand piano that was given to Mrs. Stanley by her husband. Many times the piano has been heard to play when no living person was present in the room. A night manager, for example, heard music drifting down the main hallway and went to investigate. He found that the piano melody was coming from the music room, but when he stepped inside, it stopped. Others have had similar experiences — for some reason, Flora doesn't seem to want to play when she has an audience.

F.O. and Flora aren't the only spirits active in the Stanley Hotel. Many people who have stayed there report the sounds of children playing in the hallways in the middle of the night. In many instances, this has taken place when there weren't any families with kids checked into the hotel. No one knows who these children are, but they seem to be having a wonderful time, because visitors hear the laughing, running, and romping typical of youngsters at play.

Perhaps the most haunted area of the hotel is the forth floor, which was once reserved for servants of the guests staying at the Stanley. The hallways are narrower, the rooms are smaller, and although they are very plush now, they were once very plain. Odd things happen in the rooms, which make them very popular with visitors. It would not be unusual at all to unpack your bags, walk down to the lobby to explore the hotel, then return to find that everything had been moved around in the room. According to the hotel staff, the most haunted room is 418; everyone wants to stay there, so book it well in advance of your visit.

Throughout the hotel, housekeepers make up beds only to turn their backs for a moment, then discover an imprint as if someone had just laid down. Footsteps are heard in empty hallways, doors open and close, and the room lights are turned off or on by some unseen hand. There are no "evil" presences at the Stanley, however. If anything, these are benevolent spirits that are just trying to get the attention of the human guests there. Most people find it so interesting that they return again and again.

It's a popular stop for celebrities as well. The Stanley Hotel guest book reads like a who's who. The "unsinkable" Molly Brown was a guest, as were the emperor and empress of Japan, and a string of celebrities including Elliot Gould, Brooks

Robinson, Amy Grant, Gary "Radar" Burghoff, Jerry Seinfeld, Bob Dylan, Peter Gabriel, and the cast of *Dumb and Dumber*, including Jim Carrey and Jeff Daniels.

And, of course, Stephen King. I owe a lot to the man who lit the first spark of writing in my life. I'm thankful that Mr. King stayed at the Stanley Hotel, and then wrote *The Shining*. I'm thankful that I happened into that mall bookstore in Texarkana, Texas, on the evening that I bought his book. I'm thankful that my basset hound, Fred, had to pee just as I was reading the creepy scene with the fire hose in the story. I'm thankful for so many things associated with the Stanley Hotel.

The best that I can say, though, is "thank you, Big Steve."

The Stanley Hotel
333 Wonderview
Estes Park, CO 80517
(970) 586-3371
(800) 976-1377
www.stanleyhotel.com

The Bride on the Stairs

The Lighthouse Inn — New London, Connecticut

MOST PEOPLE have heard of the beauty of Long Island Sound, or "The Sound" as it is known locally. It is bounded by Connecticut and Westchester County, New York, to the north, the Big Apple itself to the west, and Long Island to the south. The Sound is approximately one hundred ten miles long and twenty-one miles across at the widest. It is also an ecosystem known as an estuary, something I'd never heard of before. Turns out, that's a fancy word for a waterway where fresh water from rivers mixes with salt water from the ocean.

More than eight million people occupy the Sound, either through recreational or residential use. It is a significant influence, since all those people contribute about five billion dollars to its annual economy. Boating, swimming, fishing, and beach activities make up the majority of the recreational use of the beautiful body of water.

As you cruise your boat toward Connecticut, you may want to dock in the port of New London, a city founded in 1646 by John Winthrop. For many years it was known by its Indian name, "Nameaug," until 1658, at which time the General Court of

Connecticut voted to change its moniker to its namesake city of London, England. About that same time, the nearby Monhegin River was renamed the Thames. Both of these were thinly veiled attempts to placate the English Court, which held the reins on the New World at that time.

The name stuck, though — New London. While you're visiting the city, you may see an obelisk that's over one hundred and thirty feet tall. It commemorates September 6, 1781, when eight hundred British troops under General Benedict Arnold raided New London and destroyed much of the property there. They also killed eighty-four Colonial soldiers at Fort Griswold, many after the fort had been surrendered. Arnold was born in New London County, although he is definitely not a favorite son.

Also in New London is the only location in Connecticut that has been designated as a Historic Hotel of America. It was built in 1902 by steel baron Charles S. Guthrie as a summer home for his family. He gave it the name "Meadow Court" after all of the flowers that grew around the house. While we're on the subject of flowers, one of the outstanding features of the inn is the grounds, which were done by Frederick Law Olmsted, the founder of American landscape architecture.

In 1927, Meadow Court was transformed into a hotel and adopted a name for the nearby New London Harbor Light: the Lighthouse Inn. The rooms were decorated with fine antiques, and the place soon began to earn a reputation as a superior vacation destination.

There are a few other visitors who have been to the hotel over the years who still frequent the wonderful old place — at least, their spirits do.

During the 1930s, it was an extremely popular location for weddings. One reason for this is the majestic staircase that curves down into the lobby — a perfect setting for brides to make their grand entrance.

On one such festive occasion, hotel legend has it that a bride was making her way down the stairs when her feet became entangled in her dress and she tripped. To the horror of the wedding party and guests, the young lady tumbled down the rest of the way headfirst. When she came to rest at the bottom, her neck was broken.

It wasn't long before the staff and guests began to catch glimpses of a phantom woman slowly descending the staircase. Those who have seen her pause long enough claim that she is wearing a long, white wedding dress. Many believe that this lady is the bride from long ago, returning once again to walk down to the wedding that she never got to experience.

She doesn't just spend time on the staircase, however. The ghostly bride has been seen dancing through the dining room, strolling the hallways, and has even been seen in the guest rooms. Whether this is the ghost of the girl who died in the fall or some other bride returning to the scene of a long-ago wedding, she has been seen by both guests and employees of the Lighthouse Inn over the years.

The spectral bride isn't the only spirit at the hotel, however. Mysterious children have been another manifestation of the supernatural activity at the hotel. Even when there aren't any families with youngsters staying in there, kids have been heard romping and playing in the hallways — although a glance reveals that no children are present. No one knows who they are, but the voices of little girls laughing, squealing, and singing have even been heard inside guests' rooms during the night. When the occupants turn on the light to see what is going on, the room is suddenly quiet — and empty.

Some say that the girls might be a carryover from a time in the town's history when a hurricane flattened most buildings and homes, but left Meadow Court — the Lighthouse Inn — standing firm. Many families took refuge there, and one possibility is that the spirits may be returning in the form of their childhood, remembering the security of that time and place.

Others speculate that the children were once guests there who enjoyed the hospitality of the hotel and have returned there in spirit form to play once again.

When it comes right down to it, though, the identities of the children or the bride aren't all that important. You may or may not encounter them during your visit — but you will definitely have the pleasure of interacting with a friendly, attentive staff. The rooms are plush and comfortable, appointed with beautiful antiques, and have a wonderful view. Because the inn is built in a semi-circle, you're guaranteed to have a fantastic view of either the Sound or the manicured grounds and gardens of the Lighthouse Inn. After only a night there, you won't wonder at all why the hotel is so popular with its living — and a few afterlife — guests.

Lighthouse Inn
Six Guthrie Place
New London, CT 06320
(860) 443-8411
www.lighthouseinn-ct.com

The Phantom Prisoners of Pea Patch Island

Fort Delaware — Delaware City, Delaware

PEA PATCH ISLAND didn't appear on any maps or drawings of Delaware River — at least, not during the early Colonial days of the country. As the legend goes, a boat carrying a cargo of peas was heading up the river when it ran aground on the uncharted isle. It stopped with such a lurch that the peas dumped all over the island, and locals soon began to call it "Pea Patch Island."

In 1813, construction on a fort on Pea Patch Island started but was soon suspended. The strategic location of the island became more and more apparent, though, so construction began again in 1819. The masonry fort was soon completed, but only stood for about a decade. Fire destroyed it in 1831, leaving only a shell. In 1833, the ruins of the fort were torn down.

In 1848, a wave of construction began on a new structure — a pentagon-shaped fort that would cover six acres. Its walls were made of granite and brick, thirty-two feet high and up to seven feet thick in places. The fort even had a dungeon. A thirty-foot-wide moat was built around the structure, with a drawbridge on the side facing Delaware.

Two barracks were built to house the soldiers there, along with kitchens and mess halls in which to feed them. The first troops to occupy the fort were the Commonwealth artillery of Pennsylvania with the onset of the War Between the States.

On March 23, 1862, Stonewall Jackson's Confederate force struck at the Union army under the command of General Shields at Kernstown, Virginia. It was a defeat for Jackson and his men, and two hundred fifty rebel prisoners were taken to Fort Delaware. The fort was built for troops, not as a prison, so conditions for the prisoners of war were miserable. The Union saw that more inmates would be coming, so in that same year of 1862 wooden barracks were constructed to hold two thousand more. As more Confederate soldiers were captured, even more quarters were added, which took up a great deal of the island. In June of 1863, Fort Delaware had been equipped to hold ten thousand prisoners. When the Battle of Gettysburg was over, however, more than twelve thousand men were being held there. They were each allowed one overcoat or one blanket — but not both.

Water for them to use came from rain barrels at the corners of the barracks to catch water runoff from the roof. One prisoner observed, "When the rains were frequent [the water] was kept tolerably pure, but when several weeks elapsed without showers, they became putrid; the contents would appear to be fairly swarming with wiggletails and white worms."

Before the Civil war came to an end, between two and three thousand of the island's inmates died there. The fort had become known as the "Fort Delaware Death Pen." It had the worst reputation of all the Northern prisons, with the highest mortality rate in the Union.

At the end of the war the surviving prisoners were released, and the fort sat quietly until 1896 when U.S. forces occupied it again. In 1903, however, the doors swung shut yet another time.

Twice more Fort Delaware was called upon to serve as a defensive post, during World War I and again during World War II. In 1944, it looked as if America would not have to worry about an attack on her own soil, so the fort was declared to be surplus property. The defensive guns were broken down for scrap metal, and the land was deeded from federal property to the State of Delaware.

A few historically minded people saw the potential in the old place, and a movement to open it as a state park began to gain in popularity. It was restored and opened as such in 1951.

With all of the pain and suffering that went on at Fort Delaware, there are reportedly a number of spirits who still visit the place. Down in the dungeon of the fort, for example, the staff and visitors have heard the metallic sound of chains clanking, perhaps psychic impressions from a day when prisoners were incarcerated there in the most foul conditions imaginable.

There are stories of many failed escapes from the fort/prison, including a young drummer for one of the Confederate infantries. The plan was for him to feign death, and the burial detail would release him when they got outside of the walls. Most of the deceased prisoners were buried across the river at Finn's Point, New Jersey, but some say that during the most crowed times of the fort, burials were done on the island as well. As the story goes, the burial assignments for that evening were changed at the last minute, and a crew actually buried the coffin that the young man was nailed inside. It was too late when he realized what was happening, and his pounding and scraping on the inside lid of the coffin was to no avail. While walking the grounds of the island, some people have reported hearing his lamentations as his spirit still calls out to the world of the living.

When you visit the powder magazine, you may get a very strange feeling — it's more than a little creepy, but there's something more there that can't be explained. Many say that the feelings of fear and loneliness there come from the fact that James Archer, a general of the Confederacy, spent several weeks there as punishment for insurrection. He had been taken prisoner with his men at Gettysburg and imprisoned at Fort Delaware. The general had soon formulated an escape plan that started with an uprising against the Union forces there, but it failed miserably. Archer was locked in the dark, dank powder magazine that was located in the very bowels of the fort. He developed an illness while sequestered there and never recovered, so he may be continuing to stroll the place this very day.

Confederate soldiers have been seen — and even photographed — on the parade ground as if they are still serving time, and from the outside of the fort visitors have reported seeing men in uniforms peeking out through the gun turrets.

There were several escape attempts from the prison. Perhaps one of the most chilling involved several Confederate soldiers who managed to get free of the walls and swim the moat, and then tried to make it across the river. The current was much too strong, and they were pulled under with splashing and screams of terror. These sounds have also been heard from the fort, as if the prisoners were doomed to continually repeat their fate — something that most ghost hunters would classify as a residual haunting.

You can visit the fort with a short boat ride to the shore of Pea Patch Island, but check the schedules before taking a trip there — on special occasions, there are ghost tours of Fort Delaware, and there is probably no better way to see the place than with a guide who is well-versed in not only the history of Fort Delaware but the ghost stories there as well.

Fort Delaware State Park
P.O. Box 170
Delaware City, DE 19706
(302) 834-7941
http://www.visitthefort.com

The Heartbroken Bride

∞ ● ● ● ● ∞

Casa de la Paz B&B — St. Augustine, Florida

WANT TO GET my attention? Just tell me that you've discovered the fountain of youth. While I still feel very young, I tend to notice that the birthdays are ticking away much quicker that I'd like.

Oddly enough, here in the United States we actually have a place labeled "The Fountain of Youth," and it's in the city of St. Augustine, Florida, a place that claims to be the oldest city in our country.

Ponce de Leon sighted the eastern coast of Florida on Easter Sunday of 1513, landed there, and claimed it for the King of Spain. He named the land Florida, from the Spanish term for the Easter season, Pascua Florida. There was a flowing spring where he landed that de Leon assumed to be the fabled "Fountain of Youth" that he was searching for, so he drank from it in hopes of regaining the strength and vitality of his youth — as do thousands of visitors today.

Yes, that same fountain is there, and you can sample the water for yourself. But after doing so, while you're waiting for that jolt of youthful zest to kick in, there are many things to see and do in the city. Lots of shopping, more historical places to explore than you can possibly see in one trip, and even a ghost tour or two. After all, who wouldn't expect the oldest city in America to have a ghost?

When you're done for the day, a perfect place to lay down your head is a bed and breakfast called Casa de la Paz, named for the beautiful peace lily. It is a perfect complement to the history of the town, and even has a resident ghost that you might meet during your stay.

Casa de la Paz was constructed in 1915 as a private residence for a local banker named J. Duncan Puller. It was a magnificent home, with extravagant fireplaces, arched doorways, leaded glass bookcases, and interior molding that was crafted by hand — all well-befitting a banker's station in life.

From Mr. Puller, the house passed through a couple of families before being turned into a business property. The building housed a kindergarten, a restaurant, and was even carved into individual apartments. In 1986 it was purchased and lovingly transformed into the beautiful bed and breakfast that you can visit today. The opulence of the original house had once again been restored.

Many people have been guests at the inn over the years, and a few have come away with a story beyond the amenities of the B&B — you see, Casa de la Paz has a spirit that lingers there.

The story goes back to the early 1900s when the Puller family owned the house. They had guests at one time who were honeymooning and spent their first few nights as a married couple in the house. On the day that they were to leave St. Augustine, the bridegroom decided to go fishing in the waters of the Atlantic Ocean; he wasn't going to be gone all that long, so he asked his bride to wait at the inn until he returned. While he was out, a terrible storm swept in. His boat capsized and all aboard were lost.

His wife stayed in St. Augustine, grief-stricken to the point where her health began to fail her. She finally died of a broken heart.

Soon thereafter, her spirit began to appear at the house that would eventually become Casa de la Paz. It was if she were remaining there to honor her husband's request to wait for him until he returned. Several people saw her ghostly form at the house, walking the hallways and looking for her husband.

When the bed and breakfast was finally opened in the late 1980s, an open house was held for friends and dignitaries in the community. The owner gave a short speech about the history of the house, the steps taken in renovation, and so on. Afterward one of the guests remarked to him how a woman in a long skirt and big hat who was carrying a suitcase had tried to push past him to get down the stairs. The new owner just smiled and said, "Oh, you saw her too!"

Before that time, when the building had been separated into apartments, tenants reported a knock on their door and a woman's voice asking, "Is it time to leave yet?"

While the spirit of Casa de la Paz is occasionally very active, you may or may not experience her on your visit. One thing is for certain, though — whether your room looks out over the bay, the Bridge of Lions, the Lighthouse, or the courtyard of the B&B, you'll have a wonderful stay, and be rested and ready to explore the city of St. Augustine.

Now, you may be wondering — when I went to St. Augustine, did I drink from the Fountain of Youth? The answer is easy... of course I did! Since ol' Ponce is long gone, I had no aspirations that his discovery was the miraculous water that he'd thought. But I didn't want to take any chances. After all, with every tick of a birthday, I hope to find the real thing. I will be back to St. Augustine one of these days, and when I do, not only will I return to the Fountain of Youth, I'll also be staying at Casa de la Paz. Not only is it a beautiful inn, but you never know — you just might see the spirit of a young girl with a suitcase, waiting for her lover to return.

Casa de la Paz
22 Avenida Menendez
Saint Augustine, FL 32084
(904) 829-2915
(800) 929-2915
www.casadelapaz.com

A Tragedy in the Family

Forsyth Park Inn — Savannah, Georgia

THE FIRST TIME that I was exposed to the beauty of Savannah, it was in the wonderful book *Midnight in the Garden of Good and Evil* and the delightful movie that was made from it. There are two things that I soon learned, however. The first is that you have to see the city with your own eyes to truly appreciate its beauty — the historic old homes, the ancient trees laden with Spanish moss, and the breathtaking sight of the azaleas in bloom. The second thing that I quickly discovered is that Savannah has a supernatural vein running through it as deep as the roots of the old magnolia trees that grace the town.

With all of its southern charm, Savannah has come through some very rough times in its past. Founded in 1733, it was one of America's first planned cities. The streets were carefully laid out next to the Savannah River for both beauty and utility — not that far from the Atlantic Ocean. Because it was a port, its early population not only included genteel colonists, but also sailors, fur traders, pirates, and slaves.

During the American Revolution, the city was defended by Colonial forces under General Robert Howe. They were forced to flee by the superior numbers of the opposing forces, and almost a hundred lives were lost that day. The Battle of Savannah was considered an important victory for the British, giving them a stronghold in the southern colonies.

The city did not fare much better during the Civil War, when it became a battleground once again. It was considered to be Georgia's greatest port and a leading city in the Confederacy. In 1862, the Union was attempting to blockade the southern river ports and turned its attention to Savannah. By utilizing a bombardment of long-range artillery, nearby Confederate Fort Pulaski soon fell, and Savannah was overrun by soldiers from the North. General Sherman had control of the city, but it escaped the fiery fate of Atlanta.

War was not the only tragedy that befell the city, however. There have been devastating hurricanes, fires that swept through Savannah, and two horrific yellow fever epidemics — the one that occurred in 1876 claimed over one thousand lives.

It's easy to see where the spirits of Savannah may come from; turbulent times are often associated with hauntings, which would explain why so many places in town are said to be visited by ghosts.

There is another story about the city that might also shed some light on its supernatural side. An unofficial saying about the town is "Savannah was built on its dead" — a phrase coined due to the idea that some of the more historic areas of town are built on cemeteries. With the wars and other tragedies that swept through town, impromptu graveyards were established and soon forgotten. Construction sites of new buildings or old ones being restored have yielded human skeletons from the Georgia dirt, with no explanation other than at one time the property had been a cemetery.

Some think that the Savannah spirits come from the tragic days of the city, while others are convinced that these phantoms are returning to protest their final resting place being disturbed.

The ghost story that I found to be the most interesting doesn't trace back to the Revolutionary War, General Sherman's rout of the city, or even the forgotten cemeteries. The history of the haunting is well documented, with its own tragic tale; it also takes place at one of the most beautiful inns that you'll see in town!

To find it, all you have to do is locate Forsyth Park — it's a twenty-acre attraction that you definitely won't want to miss, if for no other reason than to see the massive fountain there; it's an icon from movies such as *Forrest Gump* and the aforementioned *Midnight in the Garden of Good and Evil*. The park itself was built in 1851, and is a place where time stands still. The city has worked hard to protect it from modernization, and while you might be able to scare up a game of touch football, you'll also want to walk along the paths and see the monuments and memorials to historic figures. One section is particularly special — it is the Fragrance Garden for the Blind.

As you walk through Forsyth Park, you may notice a bright yellow Queen Anne Victorian house facing it. That is our destination: the Forsyth Park Inn.

Originally, the house was built as a private residence, with its own splendid courtyard garden and a huge verandah to look out over the park. When it was constructed in 1893, I'm sure that the owners had a mental image of sipping mint juleps out on the porch as they rocked in wicker chairs and simply took in the beauty of the park.

It enjoyed different owners over the years, but in 1985 it was turned into one of Savannah's most luxurious inns. From the moment that you walk through the front door, you'll be awestruck. From the rich woodwork of the staircase to the hardwood floors that cause an echo as you walk, the best word to describe the Forsyth Park Inn is *extravagant*.

With eleven rooms and a separate cottage in the courtyard, you'll find an abundance of choices when you're making reservations. From park views and whirlpool tubs to fireplaces and other exquisite amenities, prepare yourself to be pampered.

While you're enjoying your stay, however, you may find yourself face to face with the spirit of a girl from the house's past who occasionally comes back to visit. Her tragic story is one that has the twists and turns of a Hollywood movie, yet it is true — and is the reason that the ghost of the girl named Lottie still wanders the halls of the Forsyth Park Inn.

Back at the turn of the twentieth century, a couple named Aaron and Lois Churchill owned the house. A well-to-do pair, they obviously enjoyed their home's magnificent view of the park and their opulent life in the city of Savannah. One thing was missing, however: a child.

The couple had no children, but one day a young girl named Lottie came to live with them. While we do not know the explanation that they provided to Savannah society, the girl called the Churchills "Uncle Aaron" and "Aunt Lo." They raised her as they would a daughter, giving her all the benefits of a wealthy upbringing.

When Lottie was a teenager, the family changed once again: Lois' sister Anna had fallen ill and came to stay with the family to be nursed back to health.

Lottie and Anna hit it off instantly, with Anna becoming the "big sister" that Lottie had never known. As Anna recovered, the two spent more and more time together, until they were almost inseparable. Unbeknownst to Lottie, a terrible twist to her life was brewing just below the surface of the family.

One day the young lady happened to walk in on a romantic scene where her Uncle Aaron was in an impassioned embrace with not her Aunt Lois but Anna. The adults in the house had been involved in a romantic triangle, and the sudden discovery shattered Lottie.

As much as Lottie had grown to care about Anna, she loved her would-be parents even more. She was old enough to know that the relationship would tear them all apart, so she began to fret about what to do to correct the problem.

A terrible plan was hatched.

The next afternoon when the three ladies were having their tea and cakes in the garden, Lottie secretly emptied a small vial of poison into Anna's cup. She stirred it, then sat back to watch as it performed its deadly job.

Anna gasped, then began to choke. Lois leapt out of her chair, but Anna was already dying. As the last breath escaped from her sister's lips, Lois began to sob hysterically. She cradled Anna's head, and through the tears told Lottie a secret that had been buried deep within the family: Anna was Lottie's mother. In circumstances that made her unable to care for Lottie, she presented her child to Lois and Aaron to raise as their own.

Lottie was devastated. She had killed her own mother, whom she had come to care for as a sister. The rush of information and emotion was too much for her to handle, and her mind simply snapped. The family had no choice but to commit Lottie to a mental institution where she would live out her life, and eventually die.

Her life at the house with Aaron and Lois were truly her happiest years, which may be the reason that she sometimes comes back to the inn to visit. Her spirit has been seen on the staircase, looking exactly as she did as a young lady.

Most often, though, her presence is felt out in the courtyard by the fountain, which some think was the very site of that tragic day when she took her mother's life. Lottie's ghost isn't threatening or mean-spirited — she seems to simply want to revisit the happiest time of her life. Who can blame her? If I'd grown up in a beautiful mansion like that, overlooking a lush park like Forsyth, after death I might be tempted to come back for the occasional visit as well.

The place is so beautiful that many people certainly enjoy coming back there time and time again in life!

Forsyth Park Inn
102 West Hall St.
Savannah, GA 31401
(912) 233-6800
www.forsythparkinn.com

The Return of the Queen

State Capitol — Honolulu, Hawaii

ONE OF THE most active spirits in the island chain is the monarch who used to rule the kingdom of Hawaii: Queen Lydia Liliuokalani. The story concerning how the land that she ruled turned from monarchy to statehood is one that is filled with intrigue and deception.

The spirit of Queen Liliuokalani is said to walk the ground of the capitol building today, but before looking at that, it is worth examining exactly who she was and what happened to her majesty on her journey through life.

She was born to be queen, to High Chief Kapaakea and the Chiefess Keohokalole. She was the third of ten children, and her brother would become King Kalakaua of the Hawaiian Islands.

By the age of four, she was enrolled in the Royal School where she became fluent in English and the ways of the American missionaries. She was also brought into the royal circle of King Kamehameha IV and Queen Emma.

Her brother Kalakaua took the throne of Hawaii, but upon his death in January of 1891, Lydia assumed the monarchy. As the queen, she proposed a new constitution for the islands that limited her own power. Queen Liliuokalani knew that economic considerations were pressing down on her country.

The McKinley Tariff soon began to hurt Hawaii's trade with America, though, because it infringed on the mainland market for the islands' sugar. American interests began to eye Hawaii as an additional state to bring into its sugar trade.

Queen Liliuokalani saw this coming, and in 1893 she tried to fortify the throne by issuing yet another constitution that protected both the country and her position as its monarch. A man named Sanford B. Dole, a wealthy businessman in the islands, decided to launch a campaign against the queen and enlisted the help of the American minister in the islands. Minister John L. Stephens ordered troops to take control of Iolani Palace, the queen's home, along with several other government buildings under her control. What makes this the most disturbing is that Queen Liliuokalani loved her people, treated them fairly, and was doing nothing wrong other than being caught in the middle of a trade situation with the United States involving sugar and fruit.

The next minister to Hawaii came to the island soon thereafter, representing the current American president, Grover Cleveland. After examining the situation, he determined that the people of Hawaii supported the queen and suggested to Washington that her rule be restored. In fact, he implicated the former U.S. minister as part of an illegal coup in the country.

But soon another American minister was stationed in Hawaii, and he made an overture to Queen Liliuokalani that her rule would be restored if she would only pardon those who dethroned her. She hesitated at the pressure to do this, which gave her opponents the time they needed to lobby against restoration of the queen to the throne.

They were successful. On July 4, 1894, these opponents to the monarchy announced that the Republic of Hawaii was born, and Sanford B. Dole was the first president. The United States government, eager to reestablish trade relations with Hawaii, immediately recognized the new government of the nation.

Under a very suspicious set of circumstances, Queen Liliuokalani was arrested in 1895 and was sequestered in her palace. Some people think that the fix was already in place to annex Hawaii as a state, and in 1898 a joint resolution of the U.S. Congress made Hawaii a U.S. territory. As for the queen, she passed away from complications of a stroke in 1917.

The capitol building in Honolulu that replaced Queen Liliuokalani's seat of power was designed to resemble a volcano with an open dome — specifically the "Punchbowl" on Oahu, which can be seen from the capitol building. A reflecting pool surrounds the building, representing the fact that the Hawaiian Islands are engulfed by the Pacific Ocean.

Forty pillars representing coconut palms support the roof. Historically, the trees were a source of food, water, and building materials for the people of Hawaii. On the top floor of the capitol, the support pillars are grouped into eights to represent each of the islands: Hawaii, Kahoolawe, Kauai, Lanai, Maui, Molokai, Niihau, and Oahu.

There are two entrances to the capitol, the mountain side, "mauka," and the sea side, "makai." A statute of Queen Liliuokalani was erected on the sea side, facing Iolani Palace, her home.

No one knows whether the statue brought her presence there, or whether it is simply the fact that it was the new ruling building in Hawaii, but for whatever reason Liliuokalani makes an occasional appearance at the capitol building. Both employees there and visitors to the building have reported seeing her.

One of the most famous appearances was to a little girl in March of 1982. A legislative aide was working very late one evening, and phoned her husband to come pick her up from work. He did so, bringing along their young daughter. While the girl and her father were waiting for her mother to finish up, she began playing with a tall, beautiful woman carrying leis on each arm.

The woman had on a black dress, and her hair was up on top of her head. When the mother came out, the child told her about her companion, but no one was there.

Later on, when the family attended the unveiling of the Queen Liliuokalani statue, the little girl pointed her out immediately as the woman who'd been playing with her that day.

The queen has appeared to many people, workers and visitors alike, and it is said that her visit is preceded by the smell of pungent cigar smoke, since the queen enjoyed a stogie or two in her time.

Most people agree that as badly as Queen Liliuokalani was treated as a pawn of political and financial ambition, her spirit is very kind indeed. She walks the hallways of one of the nation's most beautiful capitols, simply observing the mechanics of the new government there.

Hawaii State Capitol
415 South Bcretania St.
Honolulu, HI 96813

Maggie, the Mining Town Spirit

Historic Jameson Restaurant and Inn —
Wallace, Idaho

 IT WOULD BE hard to find a place with a more colorful past in Idaho than the town of Wallace. Heck, it might be hard to match it anywhere in the country! At one time, Wallace was known as the "Silver Capital of the World" and attracted prospectors from around the country, all looking to make their fortune there.

Of course, at that time most of the prospectors were men, so the little town of Wallace had a huge influx of the male gender in a very short period of time. When the men weren't mining, they wanted distractions, of course, so the next two industries to spring up in town were gambling and prostitution. As this all started one hundred and fifteen years ago, the township didn't have to worry about any federal entanglements by allowing these industries to prosper.

In 1889, a businessman named Theodore Jameson came to town and opened a restaurant and bar with rooms to let for the evening.

Of Theodore Jameson's establishment, the *Illustrated History of Northern Idaho*, published in 1903, proclaimed "Mr. Jameson has a good bar, always stocked with fine liquors, operates a neat and quiet billiard hall, and has his place embellished with valuable curios and collections of minerals."

As to the background of Theodore F. Jameson, the aforementioned reference says, "Our subject was educated in the public schools and when he was sixteen the family went to Missouri. He remained on the farm with his parents until he was twenty and then in 1870 we find him in San Francisco and the next year in Pioche, Nevada. In 1878 Mr. Jameson went to Leadville and there and in Rosita he engaged in the liquor business. In 1878 we see him in the famous Black Hills of South Dakota and in 1881 he went to the Wood river country, Idaho. In the fall of 1883 he was in Walla Walla, and in February 1884, Mr. Jameson came to Eagle City, Idaho. A few weeks later he went to Murray and opened a saloon. This he conducted until 1886, when a move to Wardner, whence he came to Wallace in 1889. He then opened his present place and has since given himself to his business. He is located near the business center of the city and his place is orderly and neatly equipped."

When Jameson had his bar and hotel, mining and prostitution were the two largest industries in Wallace. Men outnumbered ladies two hundred to one, and the women who were there, well, they weren't the most honorable that one might encounter. In fact, proper ladies and children did not dare enter the town without an escort.

As is the story with many old mining towns, the veins dried up and people began to leave to seek their fortunes elsewhere. The city struggled for years, but has experienced a rebirth. It is now a wonderful destination for travelers through Idaho — the city boasts many shops where guests can select from antiques, jewelry, and local items, and it is a mecca for tourists.

You can still spend the evening at Jameson's, and even get a delicious meal there, but in the course of time there have been a few spirits who have attached themselves more permanently to the place.

One of the most famous is Maggie, a female apparition who has been seen by the staff and many visitors over the years. She was a "lady of the evening" left at the hotel by a miner who promised to come back for her but never did. Legend has it that she died of a broken heart and still haunts the rooms of the Jameson today. Guests may hear her talking to herself or softly singing, or might catch a glimpse of her in the hotel hallways. Some people have reported seeing a brush, comb, or mirror show up in their room where it wasn't before, as if Maggie had been in there preparing herself to meet her beau when he returns.

While Maggie may be the most active spirit at the Jameson, there are several others, including the spirit of a man who shows up in very strange places, including a phonograph record where his reflection appeared to a startled guest.

Most everyone who works at the restaurant/hotel has a story about the old saloon. When the place is dark and everyone has gone to bed, the ghosts there have been known to raise a ruckus. Guests have even called down to complain about the noise of loud partying, even though the place is locked up tight. Some of the spirits of the Jameson just can't seem to rest.

While staying at the Jameson, you'll enjoy the city as well. A trip to Wallace is like a step back in time. Every single building downtown is listed on the National Register of Historic Places, and it holds many other honors. In 2002, it was voted as the "Best City in Idaho"; in 2003, it was ranked in the Top 30 National Towns for Prospective Second Homeowners to Find the Best Value for their Money; and in 2004, the Silver Summit 2004 declared Wallace to be the "Center of the Universe."

Sound a little extravagant for a mining town? Well, maybe it is, but you'll have a wonderful time there anyway. There are delicious restaurants to choose from, shopping that will keep you busy all during your stay, and a ghost or two that might greet you at night.

Historic Jameson Restaurant, Saloon, and Inn
304 Sixth St.
Wallace, ID 83873
(800) 556-2544

Bangers, Kidney Pie, and a Ghost or Two

The Red Lion Pub — Chicago, Illinois

I'VE NEVER BEEN to England, although I hope to make that trip one of these days. All my friends who have made the journey across the pond tell magnificent stories, although they all disagree on the best things to see and do while you're there. One thing that all of their tales have in common, though — at the risk of starting an international incident here — is that the pub food there is really, really, really bad. Never having tried the tavern cuisine in merry ole England, I can't vouch for it one way or the other.

In the name of research, however, I've visited many "English pubs" that have been established here on American soil and, quite honestly, found the normal British culinary offerings to be quite tasty. Such as the case in one of the most authentic versions that you're likely to find on this side of the Atlantic: The Red Lion Pub in Chicago.

Because the place is so old, it is replete with haunted tales. The building itself dates back to 1882, when it was on the far northern edge of Chicago out in the country. As the city spread northward, the rough Lincoln Park and DePaul sections of town engulfed the building. These were the stomping grounds of the infamous Chicago mobsters — Al Capone roamed these streets during Prohibition and John Dillinger was killed by agents from the FBI in an alley just across the street. In the post-Prohibition era the building was a bar with a reputation as wild as the neighborhood around it. The second floor was the home to an illegal gambling den, and the uppermost floor was sectioned into apartments, about which many unpleasant rumors abounded.

Through the years, the building was bought and sold time and again, and each owner tried a different business: a laundry house, a produce store, and various other shops. With each iteration, the building became more rickety and unsafe, and probably would have been condemned if not for a Windy City architect named John Cordwell. He bought the place in 1984, started the process of remodeling and restoration, then opened the English-style pub with the name "The Red Lion" — one of the most popular names for such an establishment in Great Britain between the years 1400 and 1600. The Red Lion on the sign is a derivative of the insignia of King Edward III, who ruled England during the fourteenth century. There are still almost a thousand pubs around the world bearing that name, the vast majority of which are in England.

Cordwell did an admirable job of giving the place a true British pub feel. Now that's a bold statement considering that I mentioned a few paragraphs ago that I've never actually been to England. Stepping inside makes you feel like you could be there, though — it has the atmosphere that you've seen in films and photos, and certainly matches the descriptions that my globetrotting friends have given me.

You immediately have a thousand things to look at in the bar. The fireplace and mantel are crowned by large carriage-style lamps. There are twenty years' worth of knickknacks behind the bar and on the walls, and at the far side of the room is a very red, very British phone booth. Past the bar and dining room on the first floor, you'll find stairs to take you to the second-floor dining room. On certain nights, it is used for literary readings, with theme evenings of sci-fi, fantasy, horror, and the occasional "Red Light Night" of erotic prose. Budding comedians can even find an open microphone night where they can try out their material. Out back, there is a patio and beer garden that many consider to be second to none in the city.

But what about the haunted stories that I mentioned earlier? Well, don't worry — there are plenty to be had. One of the most interesting, at least in my opinion, comes not from the history of the building but from the man who opened the Red Lion: John Cordwell. Mr. Cordwell, beloved by countless patrons of his pub, passed away several years ago. When he was initially decorating the place, however, he hung a stained glass window over the stairway to the second floor, with a memorial plaque beneath it in memory of his dad. John's father had died in England and was buried without a headstone. It was John's way of leaving a marker to commemorate his dad's life.

Once installed, people passing by it began to report a light-headed feeling, and often said that they felt the presence of a person nearby — even though no one was there. John Cordwell had the same experience, and was convinced that the spirit of his father had come to the Red Lion to show his approval of the memorial.

Another spirit is that of a dark-haired woman who frequents the second floor. Those who have seen her say that she is wearing an outfit from the Roaring Twenties. She apparently is a little mischievous, because she's credited with holding the door to the ladies room closed, effectively locking a patron in until help arrives. On one specific occasion, a female employee of the pub made a quick rest stop during her shift, but found that she couldn't open the bathroom door — it was as if it were somehow locked from the outside. After she yelled for help, another employee simply turned the door handle and it opened freely.

The sweet, sickly smell of overused lavender perfume heralds one of the other spirits from the pub. Visitors just walk into a cloud of it unexpectedly, and describe the scent as if someone's grandmother had gone completely crazy with a bottle of old-fashioned perfume. Some say that this is due to a young, special-needs woman who died in the building in the 1950s.

The downstairs bar is the home to a mysterious cowboy, rough and unkempt, who makes an occasional appearance. He speaks a curt greeting and is suddenly gone, as if he vanished right before the patron's eyes. No one knows who he is, although coincidentally the building was once a "Wild West" bar.

Hang around the Red Lion long enough, and you will hear the stories of several other spirits there: a woman who died in the downstairs restaurant area from an epileptic seizure, the ghosts of a dark-haired man and a blond-haired man who fought over a gambling debt during the days when illegal games of chance were held up on the second floor, and several more.

Almost everyone who works there — or has frequented the pub for a while — has a ghost story to tell. One of my favorites that I heard was about one of the locals who had hung around to help close the place up one evening and walked up to the second floor. It suddenly had a very unfamiliar appearance to him, as if he were looking at it during a different era. The walls were different, the furniture was different, and in the middle of the floor was the body of a young lady covered in blood. It was so terrifying a sight that he began to scream, which of course brought everyone left in the place running to see what was happening. When the owner, John, came bounding up the stairs, his friend said that everything suddenly returned to normal and the body was gone.

As I said earlier, ghost stories abound at the Red Lion, and it is worth a stop on our haunted tour of America. Along with the spirits, I have to give a nod to any place that can offer a menu with selections such as Fish and Chips, Bangers and Mash, Shepherd's Pie, Cornish Pasties, Steak and Kidney Pie, and Irish Stew. There was only one English pub staple that I didn't see that I might have wished: Scottish Eggs. I think that I'll bring them my personal recipe. Meanwhile, it's time to pull up a barstool and peruse the list of enticing brews.

The Red Lion Pub
2446 North Lincoln Ave.
Chicago, IL 60614
(773) 348-2695
www.theredlionpub.com

An Online Ghost

—«·◦●•◦·»—

Willard Library — Evansville, Indiana

AS YOU CERTAINLY know by now, I love visiting haunted places. Walking down historical hallways in the footsteps of thousands of people before me, sleeping in an antique bed, or ordering dinner at a table where someone sat a hundred years ago — all are magic to me. I also love visiting with the people who have given me so many of the stories that I have to tell about the spirits that walk this land. I can't deny, though, that as much as anything I enjoy simply sitting in those haunted places and watching what's going on around me. After all, you never know when a spirit may stroll through the room.

Imagine my surprise when, in the course of investigating places for this book, I found a place that actually has a twenty-four-hour-a-day ghost cam aimed at several locations. This makes it very easy to do a little ghost hunting right from the comfort of your keyboard!

The place is a one hundred and ten year old library located in a magnificent Victorian Gothic structure in the town of Evansville, Indiana. It is named Willard Library after the gentleman who built it, Willard Carpenter — of course, I couldn't keep from wondering why it wasn't called "Carpenter Library," but that's just me.

It holds the distinction of being the oldest operating public library in Indiana, and also boasts one of the largest circulating art book collections in the state. From the main floor reading room to the Margaret M. Maier Children's Room, you'll find that the library is a treasure trove of information. All that, and it's haunted, too.

Ghost stories at the library are well-known, and go back some sixty-odd years when one of the janitors there had an encounter with the mysterious "Lady in Gray." At the time, the building was heated by a coal furnace, so the janitor's shift started in the early morning hours when he had to go down to the basement and shovel coal into the furnace so that everything would be roasty-toasty when the staff and public arrived as the library opened. It was about three o'clock one morning as he walked into the dark room, his flashlight cutting a path in the blackness ahead, when the light illuminated a woman standing before him. She was dressed completely in gray: her dress, her shoes, even the veil covering her face. Startled, the janitor dropped the flashlight. After retrieving it, he couldn't find a sign of the woman — it was as if she had just disappeared into the darkness. As the story goes, the janitor resigned that day and never set foot in the library again.

The Lady in Gray has been seen by many others after that morning in the basement. Most often it is in an area that should be empty, yet someone from the library staff will see someone walking down one of the aisles or across a room. As they turn to see who it is, they catch a glimpse of a woman in a long, gray dress with a veil covering her face.

The spectral form isn't the only way that the mysterious woman manifests herself. Both employees and visitors have reported the sudden strong smell of perfume. It comes upon them quickly, as if some unseen person strolled into the room. One of the locations where this has occurred is the children's room, one of the hotspots of supernatural activity in the building. The scent has sometimes been accompanied by a gentle breeze of cold air.

Some of the most interesting aspects of this haunting come from the live Internet cams that have been set up in the library. At the time of this writing, three different cameras were in operation: in the research room, the children's room, and the site of the original encounter with the Lady in Gray, the basement. If they notice any anomalies in the photos, people are invited to save a snapshot from the camera, then send it to the library. There are some very interesting pictures posted on the web site under the heading "Proof." Of course, the library staff has a sense of humor, because there is also a section of the web site named "Spoof." This is where folks with a little creativity and a lot of time on their hands have published doctored photos for entertainment purposes. Ghostly entities in the "Spoof" section photos include the Three Stooges, the Stay Puft Marshmallow Man from the film *Ghostbusters*, the *Ghostbuster* stars themselves, Santa Claus, Blackbeard the Pirate, and even the King himself, Elvis Presley. With all the fun and games, though, there are some interesting images in the "Proof" section that just might be the Lady in Gray.

But who is this mysterious spirit who haunts Willard Library? There are as many stories as there are sightings of the specter. Some say that she is there because of something that happened on the property long before the building was constructed. Others speculate that it is the ghost of a woman who died there in the early days of the library, although there is no record of such a death. Perhaps the most popular theory is that the Lady in Gray is actually Louise Carpenter, Willard's daughter. She actually brought a lawsuit against the library, saying that her father was coerced into spending his money on the endeavor and that he wasn't sound of mind enough to make that decision. She lost the case, and most people felt like she had only entered into it out of greed. Louise was bitter over the defeat, so some people feel like she has returned to the library in death to claim what she could not in life.

No matter who it is, the Lady in Gray doesn't seem intent on bothering any of the flesh-and-blood people there. She is apparently content to simply walk the halls, making her presence known to an occasional lucky person who happens to be at the right place at the right time in the library… or in front of the computer even.

The web address for Willard Library is www.willard.lib.in.us, and along with all of the information that you'll find there, just click on the GhostCam button to look for the Lady in Gray yourself. Web sites come and go, of course, so if the web address has changed, a search in your favorite search engine for "Willard Library" should direct you right to it. The library has been around for over a century, and it will be around for many years to come. Who knows? The resident spirit of the Lady in Gray may continue to hang out there as well.

Willard Library
21 First Ave.
Evansville, IN 47710
(812) 425-4309
http://www.willard.lib.in.us/
http://www.libraryghost.com/

A Houseful of Ghosts

The Mason House Inn — Bentonsport, Iowa

WHEN I SAY "houseful of ghosts," I don't mean something like you may have seen in the movie *Poltergeist*. People often assume that if a place has more than a few spirits, some kind of terrible haunting must be taking place there. It's quite the opposite at the Mason House Inn; in fact, the reason that it has quite a few ghosts is that it is such a wonderful place that even in death, folks just don't want to leave!

A lot of people have passed through its door over the years. The inn was built in 1846, making it the oldest steamboat hotel on the Des Moines River. At that time, William Robinson hoped to attract steamship patrons who were traveling from Des Moines to St. Louis. To make his dream a reality, he enlisted the help of Mormon craftsmen on their way to Salt Lake City; they had stopped in Bentonsport for some time to earn additional money for the trip and restock their supplies. When his hotel was finished, Robinson named it The Ashland House and opened it for business.

The next owners, Lewis and Nancy Mason, changed the name to The Phoenix Hotel when they bought it in 1857. They couldn't make that stick, though; the folks in town began calling it the Mason House, as it would come to be known forevermore. During that time, Nancy began one of the inn's traditions: A cookie jar was placed in every guest room. The Mason family would own the inn for almost one hundred years — the last family member was Fannie Mason Kurtz, who died in front of the hotel fireplace in 1951.

The inn changed hands a few more times before the current owners purchased it. Over the course of time, it also underwent several renovations. In 1956, the owners purchased a historic train station in town and moved it beside the hotel to use as a general store. The store was joined to the inn in 1989 and remodeled to increase the number of guest rooms. In 2001, Chuck and Joy Hanson bought the Mason House and incorporated the historic post office across the street into the property.

The current owners retained the charm and authenticity of the inn — in fact, over half of the furnishings are original to the Mason family. Beautiful pieces that you'll find at the inn include a nine-foot walnut headboard, a nine-foot tall pier mirror, an eight-foot bench from a local school, a 1905 Kimball piano, an 1882 Estey pump organ, and even a Murphy copper-lined tub. One thing that you won't find is a closet — back when the inn was built, closets were taxed as additional rooms, so the builders opted for coat hooks on the wall instead.

Now, when I said that they have a houseful of ghosts, I meant it. The inn has nine guest rooms and at least five spirits wandering the halls. None bother the guests, of course, since they're all benevolent spirits.

There's one specter that guests probably won't encounter — it is an elderly woman in a long, white nightgown who has been seen up on the third floor. There aren't any rooms there that are open to the public, but family members have spotted her, and visitors in the second floor rooms have reported hearing bumping and banging up above them when the third floor should have been empty. One guest in Room 5 commented that someone in the room above spent a lot of time in a creaking rocking chair, but not only was there no one in that third floor room, there wasn't even a rocking chair there. It's now used only for storage!

A minister who was staying in Room 5 on another occasion reported that he was awakened by someone tugging on his sleeve. He was supposed to be in the room alone, so the pastor quickly jumped out of bed and turned on the light. As it turned out, he actually was there alone — at least, there were no other humans present. The minister was a confirmed non-believer in ghosts, but his evening in the Mason House Inn changed all that.

Other guests have reported a sudden chill in their room and a foggy figure materializing right in front of their eyes. Sometimes the entire figure is composed of a white mist, while on other occasions the head is clearly visible — an elderly gentleman with white hair.

Who are these spirits? Well, in the one hundred sixty year history of the place, several owners have died in the inn, including the aforementioned Fannie Mason Kurtz who passed away while relaxing in front of the fireplace. A doctor who was renting a room there during a period when the inn was a boarding house died of diphtheria. And during the Civil War, it was used as a hospital where there were almost certainly deaths from the horrible battles.

It is probably best summed up by someone with a special gift with the spirit world who visited the inn. After looking around, she said that she felt that the ghosts were happy at the Mason House and simply didn't want to leave. One didn't even die there, but had been a guest during his life and wanted to come back. She went on to say that the spirits would never hurt anyone — they just didn't want to leave the wonderful old place.

This probably explains why the ghosts there don't seem all that interested in interacting with the guests. In fact, the inn-keepers hear phantom footsteps when no guests are there, as if the "unseen visitors" are enjoying the peace and quiet of the inn. Occasionally our world and theirs intersect, though, and a visitor to the Mason House comes away with an exciting story to tell friends back home. Like an encounter with the young lad on the landing, for instance. He is reported to be about twelve years old and dressed in knickers, and enjoys playing harmless pranks on the hotel guests. Sometimes he knocks on doors, then fades away before they can be opened, or he will take an object from one room and place it in another. When the inn had old-fashioned alarm clocks, the boy had a penchant for turning them on at odd times — although now that most of the alarms have been replaced with modern digital clocks, this isn't as much of a problem.

There was a murder in Room 7 many years ago, which may explain some of the other ghostly occurrences there. A man named Mr. Knapp had been enjoying a few libations at a local tav-ern and finally made his way back to his room. As he crawled into bed, he had no idea that he'd wandered into the wrong room by mistake. The surprised guest who was already in his bed fast asleep assumed that he was being robbed, so he grabbed his walking cane and unsheathed the secret saber that it concealed. He stabbed the "assailant" through the heart, killing him in a tragic case of mistaken identity. Today, the bed in that room is sometimes found to be rumpled, as if someone were lying on it, even though the room is unoccupied. It's as if Mr. Knapp is returning to the room to have a rest — this time with no interruptions.

When you visit the Mason House, you may not get to meet one of its otherworldly inhabitants, but you will certainly have a wonderful time. The rooms are beautifully decorated in the period of the old steamboats. Some are done in traditional antique décor, while others, such as the General Store room or the Wash House room, give a whimsical peek into a bygone era. Stay in Bentonsport Room, and you'll be in what was once the inn's pub — for men only in those days, of course. At the time, curtains were not allowed on the pub's windows, so women could sneak a peek inside to see if their menfolk were there enjoying a beverage or two. If you'd like, you can even stay in the bedroom of Lewis and Nancy Mason, the inn's namesake couple. No matter what room you choose, you'll enjoy the views of the Des Moines River and the old Bentonsport Bridge, and the many shops and amenities of the town itself. It's a wonderful stop on our journey.

The Mason House Inn
21982 Hawk Drive
Bentonsport, Iowa 52565
(319) 592-3133
(800) 592-3133 (reservations)
http://www.masonhouseinn.com

The Cornerstone Ghosts

The Eldridge Hotel — Lawrence, Kansas

WHILE PASSING THROUGH the Sunflower State, if you want to find the most luxurious place to spend the evening, you don't have to go far. In the city of Lawrence, just head to the intersection of 7th and Massachusetts streets, and you'll find The Eldridge Hotel. It is a forty-eight suite, full-service hotel that the owners describe as "the most luxurious hotel in the Midwest." You'll find a romantic getaway package for couples, a pampering "ladies only" package for a weekend with the girls, and even a business retreat package for the corporate-minded. For the everyday guest there are rooms with whirlpool tubs, shopping excursions, and a restaurant and lounge that have some of the best offerings in the city. Of course, by now you must have guessed that there is something else to offer at the Eldridge: a few resident ghosts!

The hotel has a history that is every bit as fascinating as the ghost stories there — it goes back to the Civil War, when the individual states were choosing up sides between "free states" and "slave states."

When the hotel was built in 1855, Kansas wasn't actually a state but had been opened up as a territory by the U.S. government. Statehood was looming, though, and both sides of the slavery issue had their eye on Kansas.

A group named the New England Emigrant Aid Society constructed the original hotel on the site and named it the "Free State Hotel." It was an obvious attempt to make their agenda known: Kansas would join the U.S. as a free state. The role of the building was a stopover for settlers coming into the territory while they waited for their land and homes.

One very active participant in the free-state movement was a New Englander named Colonel Shalor Eldridge. In 1856, he signed a lease for the Free State Hotel and outfitted it with the finest trappings of the day. Colonel Eldridge's hotel was open for business and ready to serve the guests of the city of Lawrence.

On May 21, 1856, a pro-slavery force attacked the town. Two printing offices in town were attacked and the printing presses thrown into the river so that they could no longer be used to print anti-slavery literature. Along with the American flag, the group carried another flag, blood red in color and emblazoned with the words "Southern Rights." The mob soon turned their attentions to the Free State Hotel, shooting it with a cannon from across Massachusetts Street. They missed, reportedly due to the fact that the crew was already a little tipsy from celebrating the sacking of the town. Some of the rioters opened up on the building with gunfire but to no avail. Next, they rolled out several small kegs of gunpowder to blow up the building. The walls held once again. In desperation, they set fire to the inside of the hotel, finally succeeding in the destruction that they desired — only a shell of a building was left. The mob continued on, rioting through town, robbing stores, and creating general havoc.

Within a year, Colonel Eldridge set his mind to rebuild the hotel on the ashes of the old building. He enlisted the help of his brothers, and eighty thousand dollars later, the hotel was back in business. Eldridge was proud of his accomplishment and defiantly warned the pro-slavery movement that if they dared destroy the hotel again, he would continue to rebuild. The hotel saw an influx of people to Kansas, and the land that was only a territory became a state in 1861.

Eldridge's vow to keep rebuilding the hotel became a self-fulfilling prophecy, because the hotel would soon fall victim to Quantrill's Raiders.

A native of Ohio named William Clarke Quantrill was a staunch supporter of the slavery cause and went south to join the Confederate Army. He soon became disenchanted with the Southern forces, though, because he felt they were too soft on the Union troops. He became a renegade, gathering others of that ilk for his band of marauders, including the notorious James brothers and "Bloody" Bill Anderson. They began a campaign of raiding Kansas towns.

On August 21, 1863, Quantrill led his army of outlaws — now numbering several hundred — against the town of Lawrence. When he found that it was a headquarters for the free-state movement, he set out to literally destroy the city. In a brutal sweep through the city, his men burned every building in sight, stole everything that could be carried away, and put anyone who opposed them to death. By the end of the day one hundred eighty of the townspeople had been killed, and the town was a smoldering pile of ashes and ruin — including Eldridge's hotel.

The city was determined to rise like a phoenix, and residents adopted a motto for their cause: "From Ashes to Immortality." Once again, Colonel Eldridge set out to rebuild the hotel. Although he had originally only leased it, the place had now become a part of his soul. He found the original cornerstone from the hotel that had been destroyed and used it as part of the new building. When it was complete, he opened it with a new name:

The Hotel Eldridge. The Colonel lived in Lawrence until 1899 when he passed away at the age of eighty-two years.

Colonel Eldridge was spared the next, and final, destruction of his hotel. Although it had gained a sterling reputation at the turn of the century, and was known throughout the country for its opulence and hospitality, by 1925 the Eldridge was falling into ruin. The town decided that it was not salvageable, so it was torn down and rebuilt once again. This time the entire community stepped up to make sure that its original elegance and splendor was restored.

The hotel enjoyed a few decades of prosperity, but when the downtown district of Lawrence began to suffer, so did the hotel. It was struggling by the 1960s, and in 1970 the owners simply converted it into an apartment building. The future looked bleak, but in 1985 a group of investors took on the project of restoring the hotel once again.

When they were finished with their task, the all-suite hotel was ready to greet the public once again, its fine reputation intact.

The visitors and staff began to notice strange things at the Eldridge, however. Nothing frightening or intimidating, just a few supernatural presences that are still lurking from the hotel's past.

A good deal of the spirited activity seems to be centered around Room 506, which coincidentally enough contains the original cornerstone that Colonel Eldridge used to rebuild the hotel back in 1863. Several people have seen doors opening and closing by themselves and lights turning on and off without human assistance. Foggy breath-marks have also been seen on the mirror.

The entire fifth floor seems to have something odd about it, though. Not only have people caught glimpses of apparitions in areas where there is no one present, but there also seems to be a spirit that is especially fond of the elevator. The elevator car will rise to the fifth floor without the button being pressed, and the doors will sometimes slide open as a guest approaches. Quite honestly, it would be hard for anyone to be mad at such a service-minded spirit.

There has also been a wave of difficulties reported with guests' cameras up on the fifth floor. Often, they won't work at all even though they'd been functioning well up until the point where a guest takes them out in the Eldridge.

The ghost stories aren't limited to the fifth floor, however. In fact, cold spots have been found throughout the hotel.

I don't think that any of this is a negative thing, however. Instead, I believe that Colonel Eldridge may just be checking back in on his namesake hotel, just to make sure that everything is up to his standards.

At the Eldridge today, I'm sure that they are!

The Eldridge Hotel
701 Massachusetts
Lawrence, KS 66044
(785) 749-5011
(800) 527-0909 (reservations)
www.eldridgehotel.com

The Little Girl and the Mischievous Man

Gratz Park Inn — Lexington, Kentucky

IN OUR GHOST TOUR of America, it's time to travel to the Bluegrass State of Kentucky. There we'll stop in Lexington, at an inn that was once the first medical clinic west of the Alleghenies. What is now the laundry room served as the morgue for the patients that didn't make it.

In 1987, however, it was converted to one of the most luxurious inns that you're likely to find: the Gratz Park Inn. Its décor mirrors the 1800s elegance of the old city, and the service there is a page from the textbook of southern grace and charm.

The inn contains forty-four accommodations; thirty-eight guest rooms and six suites, all decorated with nineteenth century antique reproductions in mahogany. Stroll into the welcoming lobby, whose rose-colored fabric walls and wood floors welcome the weary traveler, and you'll be immediately impressed. You'll also notice that it is furnished in period pieces, giving you the vision of the sitting room of a stylish mansion instead of a hotel lobby.

All of the rooms are finely appointed, but the two VIP suites — the Governor's Suite and Presidential Suite — are the pinnacles of luxury. One is designed with a female touch, with vivid daffodil yellow, while the other complements it well with a masculine flair of hunter and moss green.

All the rooms are adorned with fresh flowers, and you will find toiletries from Gilchrist and Soames, along with fresh-baked chocolate chip cookies carefully laid on the bed each evening as it is turned down for the guests.

One thing that I must absolutely brag on, however, is an experience in fine dining at its best: the restaurant, Jonathan at Gratz Park. The resident chef, and man for whom the restaurant is named, is Jonathan Lundy. Hailing from Lexington, he graduated from Johnson and Whales Culinary School, but most important to me, he studied under the world famous Chef Emeril LaGasse of New Orleans. Can everyone say, "Bam!" I hesitate to even begin to talk about their selections, because there's no way to do it justice with words. Nevertheless, on one sitting you might encounter Kentucky raised pork with white cheddar grits, green beans, and maple mustard slaw. On another, you might find country ham and breaded oysters with green tomato cocktail sauce and mashed potatoes. The bottom line is that if you visit Jonathan's, get ready for a culinary feast.

When you visit the Gratz Park Inn, you may find something else that you didn't expect — a resident ghost or two. From all accounts, there may be several that continue to visit the hotel.

Although the Gratz Park Inn may have several spirits walking its halls, there are two that are its most famous: the little girl Anna and the precocious John.

Anna is a young lass who seems to be spending time at the hotel. People hear her laughing and singing, and she has been seen in the hallway of the second floor, dressed in Victorian attire and playing with her dolls as if she were waiting for her parents to come out of their room and take her for a day of sightseeing in Lexington. She's been spotted outside of the guest rooms and also near the elevators.

The staff of the hotel began to see her as soon as the hotel first opened, and it wasn't long until a guest showed up at the front desk to ask about the young girl that he'd seen playing jacks alone up on the second floor. He was concerned about her being there alone, so he spoke to the child. She looked up at him, laughed, then stood and ran around the corner. To make sure that she got back to her parents' room, he walked after her. When he rounded the corner, the little girl had disappeared; there was no way that she could have ducked into one of the guest rooms so quickly.

The workers at the hotel describe her as a cute little girl wearing Victorian attire, but with an extremely playful demeanor. They hear her romping in the hallway, singing children's songs, and have seen her playing with her toys. Sometimes she seems to even be playing with them, running into one of the cleaning closets and shutting the door. When they see this and open the door back up, of course, little Anna has disappeared — apparently she is a master at hide and seek.

If she is seen in the hotel and the staff discusses it aloud, the sightings seem to increase that week.

The hotel's other most popular ghost is called John by the staff, and he's a bit more interactive with the guests. Not content to linger out in the hallway, he will actually reset guests' alarm clocks or turn on their television sets in the middle of the night. Most guests dismiss his activities as something that they did accidentally or that was left set by a previous guest, but the staff knows better. They've heard the reports by some guests of waking up to a blaring clock or television and seeing a man sitting in one of the chairs in their room. When they turn on the light to get a better look at the intruder, mischievous John is gone — except, perhaps, for the sound of his laughter ringing through the hallway. It is said that he has a very hearty laugh that can cheer up even the most stoic of visitors.

One of the most mysterious occurrences at the Gratz Park Inn concerns the phantom fourth floor. Although the hotel is only three stories tall, guests on the top floor will occasionally call the front desk to register a complaint about all the noise on the floor above theirs: stomping about, dancing, or the sounds of a rambunctious party. The desk personnel must have a little laugh before telling the guests that there isn't a fourth floor, and the roof is not accessible.

Yet another ghost has been seen in the laundry room, the place that used to be the county morgue. This specter is a black man who walks into the room, lingers long enough to be seen, then simply fades away. No one knows who he is or what he is doing there, unless he is somehow tied to the days of the morgue.

Other spirits that have been seen are that of a sad-looking man walking the lower hallways and a woman in a white dress and hat.

All that said, my vote is to spend some quality time in Jonathan's. You may not find a ghost there, but you'll find a meal that will cap off a perfect trip to this historic old hotel.

Gratz Park Inn
120 West Second
Lexington, KY 40507
(800) 752-4166
www.gratzparkinn.com

A Fiendish Doctor and His Restless Victims

The LaLaurie Mansion — New Orleans, Louisiana

photo by Kriss Stephens

NEW ORLEANS. The Crescent City. The Big Easy. By any of these names, the city is just as wonderful a place. There is something for everyone: Sinner or saint, you can find entertainment there twenty-four hours a day.

The hardest thing about writing this chapter is trying to reign myself in so that this doesn't become its own two hundred-page travel guide… and believe me, as much as I love New Orleans, it could *easily* go in that direction.

Instead, let me just give you a few quick things that are requirements for your visit there, at least in my humble opinion.

First of all, stay in one of the wonderfully historic hotels in the French Quarter. Sure, they cost a little more, but save up your pennies and you'll find that it's well worth the extra few dollars. Not only can you walk to most of the places that you'll be visiting on your trip, but you'll also find that the hotels in the Quarter are often haunted as well.

For breakfast, go to Café du Monde for strong chicory coffee and beignets. There will probably be a crowd there, so don't stand in line to get a table. Go to the take-out window instead, get what you want, then find a place to sit on the concrete wall beside the restaurant to enjoy those delicious pastries covered in powdered sugar. It's a New Orleans tradition, so don't dare skip this ritual.

As to the rest of your meals, well, if you're in the French Quarter it's hard to go wrong. We tried several places where we just walked in off the street, and everything was delicious. Of course, we dined at some of the better-known places as well — The Court of Two Sisters is definitely worth a visit.

I find myself running out of room here. With that in mind, I'll simply say: Go to the zoo, and take the street car to get there; stroll along the crescent walk beside the mighty Mississippi; drink a Hurricane at Pat O'Brien's; take a look at the famous cemeteries but only on a tour with a guide; visit the aquarium; and, of course, have your fortune told in front of St. Louis Cathedral.

Before I leave the food theme behind, be sure to eat at The Clover Grill one evening — you can get an unbelievably scrumptious burger cooked under a genuine Cadillac hubcap. Also, make sure that in the course of things you get a Lucky Dog, which is a hot dog from one of the carts on Bourbon Street shaped like — what else — a hot dog.

Whew! I've been rambling on like a travel agent after a double cappuccino with extra cream. I'm not even sure why; after all, I'm just as passionate about most of the cities in this book. There's just something about New Orleans that is too exciting not to share.

When it comes to the supernatural side of the city, well, it would be harder to find a place in the French Quarter that *isn't* haunted. Many of the hotels there have ghosts roaming the hallways, as do restaurants and boutiques alike. I wouldn't know where to begin when it comes to haunted places in New Orleans.

Okay, that's not quite true. There is one place that we ran across on our travels around the Quarter that had quite a chilling tale to tell. My only quandary about including it in this chapter was that it is not accessible to the public. By reading the rest of this book, or any of the others I've written, you probably know that I like to write about places that you can go visit for yourself. Otherwise, I'm just spinning yarns that can't be verified, and there's nothing that I like more than hearing back from my readers about their own experiences at places in my books.

The location that I'm talking about defies simple explanation. It is definitely privately owned, though, so I would ask you to please respect the privacy of the people who live there. That said, let's take a stroll down Rue Royal in the French Quarter for a look at LaLaurie Mansion.

I first heard about it on a carriage tour of the Quarter, when the driver told my wife and me horrific stories about the building's past — and although he said that the troubled spirits occupying the house seemed to have settled down, it nevertheless is one of the darker chapters in the city's history.

Dr. Louis LaLaurie and his wife, Madame Delphine LaLaurie, purchased the mansion at 1140 Royal Street from Edmond Soniat du Fossat in1831. They furnished it with the finest furniture and trappings from Europe and hung crystal chandeliers from the lofty ceilings. The wealthy couple soon became the darlings of the New Orleans social scene, and were hobnobbing with the elite of the city. Lavish parties were hosted at their home, where the guest list was a virtual "who's who" of New Orleans aristocracy. Soon there was no couple in the Quarter as respected as the LaLauries.

People who spent time with them soon discovered that Delphine had a cruel streak, however — especially when it came to her slaves. Her cook was kept chained to the kitchen fireplace so that she could not leave her station — nor could she escape the grueling heat. Delphine was once witnessed chasing a young slave girl across the roof of the mansion, trying to lash her with a whip. In her attempt to escape, the young girl fell to her death. Madame LaLaurie had her body quickly collected, then buried in secret to try to avoid any trouble.

There were witnesses in the street below, however, and the authorities were called. Madame LaLaurie was fined for the incident, and the couple's slaves were seized to be resold at auction.

She would not accept defeat, however, and had family members attend the sale and buy the slaves back for her. No one knew the terrible fate that awaited those poor souls.

On April 10, 1834, a fire broke out at LaLaurie Mansion, and the local fire brigade descended on the house to try to extinguish it. It had started in the kitchen, and even though it spread they were able to deal with it quickly and efficiently. As the firefighters inspected the rest of the house to make sure that it hadn't spread, they came upon a mysterious armored door in the attic. Wanting to be thorough, the firemen broke down the door — and found a terrible scene inside.

The air that escaped from the room had the pungent odor of death and decay. Many of the firemen began to vomit and even pass out from the smell. Those who were able to continue inside could not believe the sights before them. The room was a real-life chamber of horrors. Crude operating tables were stationed about the room, as were cages that were barely large enough for a human being. A female slave whose arms and legs had been amputated was strapped to one table — she was little more than a thrashing torso. Yet another slave had obviously been the victim of a cruel experiment where her arms and legs had been intentionally broken, then set back at odd angles, giving her a crab-like appearance. Body parts littered the floor in various stages of decay, and there were many bodies of slaves who had mercifully died. Severed heads were found with holes in the skulls, as if they had been opened with some type of utensil to examine — or stir around — the brains inside. Some bodies were chained to walls, and many had been mutilated beyond recognition. Still others appeared to have had their limbs stretched for some torturous cause known only to the LaLauries.

Word of the atrocities quickly spread through the French Quarter, and the people of New Orleans quickly turned on the once-prestigious couple. A mob formed outside of the mansion demanding vigilante justice — some had even brought their own ropes that were fashioned into hangman's nooses.

The gates to the mansion suddenly burst open, and a carriage came thundering through the crowd. Doctor and Madame LaLaurie escaped that night, and rumors began to spread that they had fled to France.

The grisly task of removing the tortured slaves began, and even more horrors were discovered. When the house had been emptied, the people of the Quarter stormed the mansion in a fit of mob hysteria and rage. For thirty years afterward, it sat empty, falling deeper into a spiral of ruin and decay.

Rumors began to spread about the place. Reputable people reported screams from the empty building, and vagrants who chose to spend the night there were said to simply disappear into the bowels of the house. Passers-by reported seeing faces in the window and the tortured spirits of the mutilated slaves walking through the house.

In 1865 the house was remodeled in an attempt to save and reoccupy it. The new owner lived there for only a matter of months before abandoning the property. There was a parade of businesses that tried to occupy the old LaLaurie house: a barber-shop, a furniture store, a girls' school, a bar, and even a dance school. None lasted, and the spirits of the mansion were always blamed.

There were several people who tried to turn the house into a residence again, but to no avail. Spectral phantoms were reported to walk the hallways, and the sights, sounds, and smells of the long-ago horror continued to play out for the new owners. The house was once again empty.

For whatever reason, the supernatural activity there seems to have quelled. A retired New Orleans physician purchased LaLaurie Mansion and restored the home to its original beauty — with no supernatural experiences to report. Perhaps the spirits are finally at rest.

But what became of Doctor and Madame LaLaurie? No one knows for sure, although there are rumors. Some legends say that they did actually flee to Paris, while there are other stories that the couple went no further than St. Tammany Parish in Louisiana, where they lived on the north shore of Lake Ponchatrain.

An odd discovery occurred in 1941, however. In St. Louis Cemetery #1 a grave marker was discovered for the tomb of Madame LaLaurie. It had become dislodged from the crypt, so the actual resting place of Delphine may never be known — nor the fate of her husband, the fiendish doctor who disappeared with her into that terrible April night.

LaLaurie Mansion
1140 Rue Royal
New Orleans, LA 70116

The Gourmet Ghosts

━━━━━⋅●◆●⋅━━━━━

The Kennebunk Inn — Kennebunk, Maine

DURING THE FIRST George Bush's term as president, I must have heard the name Kennebunkport, Maine, a hundred times. Walker's Point was the seaside home and official retreat of former President George Bush. He hosted many foreign dignitaries there, worked on national policy within those walls, and, occasionally, just spent a few days getting away from the stress of the office.

When I was looking around for an interesting place in Maine with a good ghost story or two, imagine my surprise when I found the city of Kennebunk. My first thought was, "That's where former President Bush has his house, but someone's misspelled the name — it's supposed to be Kennebunkport!" As it turns out, that wasn't the case at all.

Both Kennebunk and Kennebunkport are cities just down the Kennebunk River from each other, and have quite a bit in common. You'll even see them referenced as the "Kennebunks," both year-round tourist destinations.

The early history of the area contains a fact that few people in the nation today know: Maine was once a part of the state of Massachusetts. When it was joined together, the people there began to have rumblings in 1770 about separation because it was so difficult and expensive to send representatives to the state government in Boston. Because it was separated from Massachusetts proper, many of the laws enacted for the state as a whole seemed to be unfair to those in the northeasternmost territory. After many problems and much debate, Maine sent its bill for statehood to Congress in December of 1819. Although there was much controversy surrounding the split, Congress passed it in 1820, and the state of Maine was born.

By that time, the settlement of Kennebunk was already established — Europeans had been there since the 1600s, streaming to the New World seeking their fortune. Because homes and businesses were springing up all over the new colonies, there was a huge demand for lumber. The vast forests of the northeast were the perfect resource from which to draw, so sawmills began to spring up in the area; timber harvesting became a thriving business in the area that would become the city Kennebunk.

At that time, it was a part of the city of Wells, but it separated into its own town in 1820, the same year that Maine was granted its statehood. Because the town was situated on the Kennebunk River, just upstream from the mighty Atlantic Ocean, people there became skilled shipbuilders and fishermen.

In 1799, a physician named Dr. Phineas Cole built a home in the city for his family. It was a showplace befitting his status, and a year later a barn was added behind the house. Over the next hundred or so years, the house passed through several owners. Each added their own touches to the house, but more importantly, they helped to preserve the integrity of the structure and the property.

In the 1920s, the house and the barn were joined together and the building opened for the first time as an inn named The Tavern, which served the ever-increasing tourist trade in the Kennebunk area.

Twenty years later things were going so well that it was purchased by an innkeeper named Walter Day, who expanded to a full sixteen rooms and changed the name to the Kennebunk Inn, the moniker that it holds to this very day. More rooms were added in 1980 by a new owner, Arthur LeBlanc, and the reputation of the inn continued to grow.

Today, the Kennebunk Inn has twenty-six rooms and suites, each one with a distinctive personality. You'll find antique porcelain bathtubs supported by claw feet, furniture from a bygone era of the nation, and four-poster beds just begging for a guest to snuggle down under its warm, soft quilts.

An added bonus of staying at the inn is that the current innkeepers are not only skilled in the fine art of pampering their guests, but they are also classically trained chefs who are as passionate about their cuisine as they are about their inn. Until you can actually arrange your trip there, just enjoy the description from the inn's web site:

> *"Consider as a first course Shrimp and Andouille*
> *Sausage Etouffee, sautéed and cooked in classic New*
> *Orleans style over croutons, followed by a main course of*
> *Pan Seared Casco Bay Day Boat Cod with mashed*
> *fingerling potatoes, haricot verts, red onion marmalade*
> *and pomegranate buerre blanc, and for dessert, a*
> *Signature S'more — a square of chocolate pate topped*
> *with homemade marshmallow on a graham cracker crust*
> *accompanied by the requisite "shot" of cold milk."*

If just reading that doesn't make your mouth water, then as we'd say in my hometown, something's bad wrong with you! After dining at the Kennebunk Inn, you can take advantage of the many things to do in town: shop for antiques, browse the museums and galleries, walk the beaches, and even take a fishing excursion or lobster boat cruise.

While you're staying there, be sure to keep an eye open for any ghostly activity. There have been many reported incidents through the years, many of which have taken place in the dining room and pub. On one occasion, a member of the waitstaff was carrying a tray of wineglasses when one jumped off and flew to the floor — this event was witnessed by several people, and it definitely wasn't an ordinary fumble by a waiter. It was as if some unseen hand had knocked that single glass from the tray on purpose.

This is not some isolated event, though. Glasses have jumped off the shelves from behind the bar in the same manner, often falling across the room in defiance of the laws of gravity.

Cold spots have also been encountered in the Kennebunk Inn, an earmark of most haunted places. But who are these spirits that are returning to visit? Some people feel that it is the ghost of one of the former owners, intrigued by the new additions to the property. There are other folks who are convinced that the spirited activity is the responsibility of a man named Cyrus, a night clerk who worked at the inn for many years.

Whoever they are, these benevolent spirits seem content with their occasional visit, if only to let the people of our time know that they're still around to check up on things. If that's the case, then I am sure they're impressed with the quality of cuisine that is currently being served at the Kennebunk Inn. The flesh-and-blood visitors certainly are!

Kennebunk Inn
45 Main St.
Kennebunk, ME 04043
(207) 985-3351
www.TheKennebunkInn.com

Oyster Shooters and a Pesky Poltergeist

Middleton Tavern — Annapolis, Maryland

I DID AN OYSTER shooter in a restaurant in Dallas, Texas, one evening. It was, well, anticlimactic. A rubbery oyster floating in a shot glass of beer was a little tough to get down, even doing it shooter-style. The waitress came back to our table and said, "Well, you're all done! Would you like another one?"

No thanks. I'm done. Forever.

Since then, I'm a little leery of restaurants that feature oyster shooters. Imagine my surprise when I started making inquires about Middleton Tavern up in the Naval Academy's hometown: Annapolis, Maryland. I heard all sorts of food recommendations: Cuban Black Bean Soup, Steak Diane, Broiled Rockfish, Smoked Chesapeake Bluefish, Oysters Rockefeller, and, of course, Oyster Shooters. When I balked at that last item and explained why, I was told that you never, ever, ever try one in a landlocked city — and maybe that's something to consider.

As it turns out, Middleton Tavern is one of the favorite places in Annapolis to shoot these slippery little creatures. Its reputation for history is as impressive as its menu, something else that I loved about the place.

The Tavern is one of the city's eighteenth-century buildings, something that Annapolis has more of than any other city in the country. It was originally built somewhere around 1740 in a classic Georgian style.

Horatio Middleton purchased it in 1750, and opened his tavern there. To supplement the income, he also ran a ferry between Annapolis and Rock Hall on the eastern shore. The law at that time dictated that anyone operating a ferry must also provide overnight lodging for travelers, so he opened an inn as part of his tavern. Taking Middleton's ferry cut a considerable amount of time off of the journey between Virginia and Philadelphia, so it was a very popular mode of travel. Some of the founders of our country rode the ferry: George Washington, Thomas Jefferson, James Monroe, and Benjamin Franklin. Legend has it that they stopped in at the tavern for a pint of ale, and occasionally broke up their trip by spending the night at the inn.

Middleton Tavern was also a popular meeting place for organizations such as the Tuesday Club, whose main purpose seemed to be partying — they gathered at Middleton's to eat, drink, smoke, and gamble. The Maryland Jockey Club and the Free Masons also used the tavern as a place to meet.

Horatio Middleton eventually died, and operation of the tavern was continued by his wife. Later his son took over the duties, including the ferry, and he even expanded his father's operation.

Through the years the building had several different owners. The name changed, as did the business there. In 1968, it was purchased by the current owner and the Middleton name restored. When you visit there, you'll find it decorated with a flair from its colorful and historic past. There are two fireplaces that are certain to take the chill out of the cold air blowing off of the water. You'll also find a piano bar upstairs where you can relax with a frosty glass of Samuel Middleton's on tap. You may also run across the tavern's resident ghost, Roland.

The folks at Middleton's consider Roland to be a poltergeist — a "noisy ghost." He is not some feared phantom or unwelcome specter, however. Roland is instead a welcome member of the unofficial staff.

He is known for moving tables and chairs around occasionally, rearranging them when no human is present. He also tosses glasses and plates when the mood strikes, giving the tavern staff fits. Glasses have been knocked off of the bar shelves when no patron or employee is even near. Some have caught a quick glimpse of Roland — a man in patriot-era clothing gazing out across the harbor. Most often, however, people detect his presence by the smell of cigars, which are not allowed in the dining room. Roland seems to love them, and he isn't bashful about strolling the restaurant while puffing on a phantom stogie.

But who is this spirit dubbed "Roland" by the folks at Middleton Tavern? Could he be old Horatio Middleton himself, keeping an eye on the place that he founded over two hundred and fifty years ago? No one knows his actual identity, only the fact that he does continue to frequent the tavern. If you visit there, keep your eyes — and nose — open to the possibilities of his presence.

But what about those oyster shooters that the tavern is so famous for? Well, they're much more interesting than you'd think; certainly more so than the one I'd downed that day in Dallas. At the Middleton Tavern, you are given a shucked oyster smothered in the special cocktail sauce in a shot glass. If you're feeling a little adventurous, you can even have pepper vodka added to the shot glass. Right beside it is a small shooter of cold beer to chase it with. Sound interesting — you bet. Pick up your oyster shooter, put it to your lips, then toss back your head. After that little hunk of seabeast slides down your throat, grab your shooter of cold beer and toss it down as well. Ahhhhh.... welcome to Middleton Tavern!

Middleton Tavern
2 Market Space
Annapolis, MD 21401
(410) 263-3323
www.middletontavern.com

Lizzie Borden Took an Axe...

The Lizzie Borden Bed & Breakfast — Fall River, Massachusetts

THERE IS AN old rhyme that most of us learned in our childhoods — one that freaked our parents out every time they heard us singing it:

> *Lizzie Borden took an axe*
> *And gave her mother forty whacks.*
> *Once she saw what she had done,*
> *She gave her father forty-one.*

It refers, of course, to the horrible double homicide that occurred in Fall River, Massachusetts, on August 4, 1892. Andrew Borden and his wife, Abby, had both been murdered in a heinous crime. Andrew's daughter Lizzie would be accused but finally acquitted of the crime.

George D. Robinson, the lead defense attorney for Lizzie, summed up the case like this: "*...one of the most dastardly and diabolical crimes that was ever committed in Massachusetts... Who could have done such an act? In the quiet of the home, in the broad daylight of an August day, on the street of a popular city, with houses within a stone's throw, nay, almost touching, who could have done it?*"

He went on to describe the condition of Abby Borden's body: "*Inspection of the victims discloses that Mrs. Borden had been slain by the use of some sharp and terrible instrument, inflicting upon her head eighteen blows, thirteen of them crushing through the skull; and below stairs, lying upon the sofa, was Mr. Borden's dead and mutilated body, with eleven strokes upon the head, four of them crushing the skull."*

The case against Lizzie was mostly circumstantial, although there were a few very suspicious, if not downright incriminating, items that surfaced in the trial.

The day before the murder, Lizzie's stepmother went to the doctor claiming that she and her husband had both been poisoned during the night. Because the symptoms were only nausea and vomiting, the doctor sent her home with orders to simply rest.

A clerk from a local pharmaceutical shop told police that Lizzie had been in the store that day asking to buy a poison named prussic acid. The clerk had refused to sell it to her since she did not have a prescription. Two additional witnesses placed Lizzie in the store during that time period. She denied trying to buy the poison or even visiting the pharmacy, although she did admit that she had been out that morning. Lizzie later changed her story to say that she didn't leave the house at all until the evening.

In addition, a neighbor saw the accused burning a dress a few days after the murder. The neighbor told her, "If I were you, I wouldn't let anybody see me do that, Lizzie." Miss Borden replied that it was a dress stained with paint that needed to be disposed of. No one knows why she didn't simply throw it away.

Her skillful lawyers were successful in removing these items from the trial, a fact that contributed greatly to her acquittal. The crime remains unsolved to this day, although most experts feel that Lizzie was the guilty party.

Later in her life, she was ostracized by the people of Fall River, and lived in near-total seclusion. She was rarely seen, and hardly ever interacted with the public.

One authoritative examination of the case was done by Robert Sullivan in his book *Goodbye Lizzie Borden*. In it, he interviewed the niece of Abby Borden, Lizzie's stepmother who was murdered. The niece told a story about Lizzie that doesn't bode well for her innocence. Apparently Lizzie Borden was entertaining guests one day before the killings occurred, when her stepmother's cat kept pushing the door to the room open and interrupting their conversation. She picked up the cat and took it down to the basement, where she placed it on a chopping block and lopped off the poor animal's head. Days later when her stepmother was wondering where the cat had gone, Lizzie told her to go down to the basement and she'd find the kitty. Abby Borden did just that, and found the horrific sight of the dead and decaying cat. Soon, she would suffer the same fate as her pet.

The Lizzie Borden case intrigued America, and even to this day speculation continues. The case has been the catalyst for many books, plays, movies, television shows and reenactments, a musical, and even a ballet. Still, according to the law, Miss Borden died an innocent woman.

Today, the home where the murders were committed has been faithfully restored and opened to the public as a tour home and bed and breakfast. You can spend the night in the house, and even sleep in one of the rooms where the murders occurred. Visitors can explore the home to draw their own conclusions as to what might have happened on that day over a century ago. For your morning meal, you are even treated to a breakfast much like the Borden family would have eaten on that fateful day. As well as being an authentic period meal, it is delicious as well — Boston's "Phantom Gourmet" gave it the highest rating.

But visitors to the Borden home aren't necessarily the only ones present — for some time, people have been having haunted encounters with spirits there. Both the staff and the inn's guests report that when the home is quiet, the faint sound of a woman crying can be heard. Some speculate that it couldn't be Abby Borden, one of the victims. Because of the blood patterns, it is believed that the first blow killed her — while she may have seen her assailant, it is doubtful that she suffered. The crying may belong to Lizzie herself, sobbing over the incidents of that day.

Phantom footsteps are also heard in the house, which have been attributed to the spirits of Andrew and Abby Borden. They walk from room to room in the house, tracing the paths that they walked in life.

A full-form apparition also makes an occasional appearance: that of an elderly lady in Victorian dress. She seems to be going about the business of housekeeping: tidying the rooms, dusting the furniture, and straightening the beds. A few visitors have even awakened during the night to see her tucking the covers around them.

There is another occurrence that has been reported at the inn also concerning the beds — guests see the covers smooth and flat, but when they look back, there is an impression there as if a human has laid down. In some cases the guests have straightened the bed covers back out, only to see the impression again.

While there is no guarantee that a visit to the Lizzie Borden Bed and Breakfast will produce an encounter with one of the ghosts who frequent it, I can assure you of one thing. When you're walking through the rooms of the Borden home, you can't help but feel a chill from its bloody past. Oddly enough, though, it is more interesting than frightening, and is an experience that you will remember for a very long time.

The only thing that you won't be able to do is to fall asleep without hearing a little voice in your head softly singing, "Lizzie Borden took an axe, and gave her mother forty whacks..."

The Lizzie Borden Bed & Breakfast
92 Second St.
Fall River, MA 02721
(508) 675-7333
www.lizzie-borden.com

The Lightkeeper's Ghost

Old Presque Isle Lighthouse — Presque Isle, Michigan

ON ONE OF my trips to Michigan, a friend who lived in Mount Pleasant was giving me directions. "We're basically in the middle of the glove," he said. I'd never thought about it, but I guess that makes a lot of sense, because the larger part of the state is indeed shaped like a right hand — or, I guess, a glove. Using that same analogy, our next stop is located more or less where the tip of the glove's index finger would be.

Glancing at a map, Presque Isle looks like a small island off the coast of Michigan on the eastern shore of Lake Huron. It's actually not, though — instead it's something like a peninsula. Still, Presque Isle harbor became an important location for captains sailing their vessels on Huron.

As early as 1800, French trappers used the natural harbor for shelter from the potentially dangerous waters of the lake. They're the ones who named the place Presque Isle, meaning "almost an island."

A few decades later, as ships powered by steam began to sail Lake Huron, captains pulled into the harbor to add to their supply of wood from the land around the lake or seek refuge from the harsh storms that could arise with little warning. It is said that if a storm was brewing on the lake and a captain saw that he couldn't make Presque Isle, he would simply turn around and head back to his homeport.

The harbor became such an important maritime interest that a state representative named Isaac Crary asked Congress for funds to build a lighthouse there. Congress recognized the need and appropriated five thousand dollars for the lighthouse to be built.

Construction was begun in 1839; when finished, the tower stood thirty feet high and had an eighteen-foot base with four-foot thick walls. A spiral stairway wound to the top that housed the lantern and lenses. A lighthouse keeper named Henry L. Woolsey was the first person to man the lighthouse, which was first fired up on September 23, 1840.

The light had served the sailors of Lake Huron for over twenty years when it was determined that the keeper's house was in such disrepair that it would have to be torn down and rebuilt. The money was allocated but was never spent — at least not to improve the residence. In 1868 it was determined that the lighthouse's placement could be better, so a much larger light was proposed by the Lighthouse Board. Construction started about a mile to the north, and the Presque Isle Lighthouse — or Old Presque Isle Lighthouse, as it came to be known — was abandoned. The lens and lantern were removed, and the beacon sat empty for almost twenty-six years.

The lighthouse was finally put up for auction, and the first in a long chain of owners took it over. Some were entrepreneurs, hoping to make a buck on the place; others just wanted use of the land; and still others had an eye for preserving the history of the Old Presque Isle Lighthouse for future generations. The Stebbins family would hold the property for some time, starting with Bliss Stebbins who bought it for seventy dollars at the turn of the twentieth century in a tax sale. He never developed the land as he'd hoped, so he sold it to his brother Francis in 1930. Francis B. Stebbins was the first person to see the historical potential of the lighthouse, and he began to give tours to anyone interested in seeing the place. He also repaired the light so that it would shine once again, which it did until the Coast Guard made him extinguish it so as to not confuse ships coming into the harbor. Just to make sure that he didn't get the urge to crank it up again, they removed the machinery that rotated the light and lens.

From Francis, the property passed to his son Jim Stebbins, who took his father's vision for the lighthouse even further — he began to assemble a full-blown maritime museum in the keeper's house, and officially opened it up for tours. He even had an idea for a "step back in time" tour, and hired college girls from the area to be the docents. They dressed in costumes from the 1800s, and were so beautiful that the main customer demographic became college boys looking to meet the girls and spend time with them, so in 1977 Jim abandoned that idea and hired a retired couple to take over the place: George and Loraine Parris.

George and Loraine became the official keepers of the property, even though they didn't actually own it. While Loraine worked in the museum, George gave tours of the lighthouse. He enjoyed playing pranks on the visitors and showing them a good time — his favorite trick for quite some time was the "Foghorn Test of Strength." He would ask for volunteers who thought that they could stand in front of the mighty horn as he set it off. No matter how rigid a stance the person took, George would blow the horn and the vibration would knock them clean off their feet.

George loved the people who visited the Old Presque Isle Lighthouse, and the people loved him. Many came back season after season just to see what tricks and tales George had cooked up lately. On January 2, 1992, a single day after celebrating the

New Year, the most beloved man in Presque Isle, Michigan, died of a heart attack. A chapter in the lighthouse's history had been closed — but perhaps a new one had begun.

As Loraine was driving to the property on Grand Lake Road, which had a clear view of the lighthouse, she saw that it was illuminated. She knew that the Coast Guard had rendered this impossible, but there it was before her. By the time that she arrived at the keeper's house, though, everything was dark.

The next day she climbed the steps of the lighthouse to make sure that everything was in order, and she saw that there was no way that someone could have turned the light on. Yet, this same pattern repeated itself again and again. Loraine never said anything about it because she thought that people might think her crazy.

Soon other folks began to see the light, however — a yellowish glow was reported from the lighthouse by several people. Some thought that the light had been put back into operation, but others drove out for a closer look, only to find that it was dark once again.

It was even spotted by members of the Air National Guard, who flew a few missions over the area, and by the Coast Guard, who investigated to make sure that no one could fire the light back up. It had been permanently disabled years before, so there was no way that the light could be shining. Yet it was.

Many people believe that the spirit of playful old George is occasionally paying a visit to the lighthouse that he loved so much, just to let folks know that he's doing just fine and to keep alive the stories of the lighthouse that he loved so much.

Old Presque Isle Lighthouse
5295 Grand Lake Road
Presque Isle, MI 49777
(989) 595-2787

A Penny-Wise Ghost

— ◦ ● ◉ ● ◦ —

Thayer's Historic Bed 'n Breakfast —
Annandale, Minnesota

FOR OUR NEXT STOP, please direct your attention up toward the state of Minnesota, the "Land of 10,000 Lakes."

In central Minnesota's Heart of the Lakes region you'll find the city of Annandale, which is home to a very historic inn — Thayer's Bed 'n Breakfast, which is advertised as being "no ordinary B&B." It is also the home to some resident ghosts, including the spirits of the first innkeepers, Gus and Caroline Thayer. Now, Gus is one of those people whose life was interesting and colorful. With a big heart and an adventurous soul, it's no wonder that death hasn't slowed him down all that much.

Albert Augustus Thayer, or simply "Gus" to his friends, was a native of Michigan who was born in 1848 just a few days after Christmas. His relatives had come to America on the *Mayflower*. He always had a daring side, so when he was a boy he lied about his age so that he could serve in the Civil War. Young Gus became a drummer for the Seventh Volunteer Infantry in 1864.

A few years after the war was over in 1870 he married a woman named Mary, and together they had two children. She passed away four years later, however, and Gus was left a widower.

After another four years, in 1878, Gus had met another woman and fallen in love. Miss Caroline Hill became the next — and final — Mrs. Thayer. Their original home was in Osseo, Minnesota, but Gus moved the family to the city of Fair Haven in search of greater opportunity. They stayed there for fifteen years, but as the grass began to grow under Gus's feet, he moved the family once again, this time to Annandale.

The couple became innkeepers at one of two hotels in town, the Annandale Inn. They must have learned the business inside and out, because in 1895 they approached the Soo Line Railroad for a loan to build another hotel in town. During that time Gus had many additional jobs, including town constable, mill operator, and thresher, but he was obviously ready to tackle the job of running a hotel of his own.

The railroad liked the idea of having another place for travelers to stay, so the deal was struck and Thayer built his luxury hotel. It was a place where people could have a good meal, enjoy an evening of dancing and libations, and then go to their room to turn in for the evening.

The inn prospered, and over the years it served visitors to Annandale well. It changed hands several times, and now rests in the capable and attentive hands of innkeeper Sharon Gammell, one of the most delightful people in the world. I could literally sit and talk with her for hours. I get the feeling — how does that old saying go? — that there are no strangers to Sharon, only friends she hasn't met.

When she and her husband first looked at the inn, Sharon told me that she went upstairs alone to look around. On the third floor, she could literally feel the presence of the spirits. She announced to whatever presences might be at the inn, "I don't know who you are, but you will be respected in this house." From that point on, she's had a wonderful working relationship with the ghosts there.

One of the active entities there is old Gus himself, and he has a unique way of making his presence known — he leaves pennies for the guests. Pennies are a sign of encouragement; Gus uses them as an acknowledgement that he recognizes your presence there, and wants you to be aware of him. For newlyweds, he often leaves a penny on the threshold as a special greeting for their stay.

There are other spirits at the inn as well, but they all get along wonderfully with Sharon and the staff. Sometimes as one of the waitresses is passing from the kitchen to the dining room with a full tray of food, the door will swing open by itself — a welcome helping hand for seasoned employees but often a shock to anyone new on the staff.

That's the nature of the spirits at Thayer's, though — friendly, playful, and seemingly proud of Sharon's efforts there.

She can share any number of ghostly encounters that have happened over the years, but there are a few that are absolute favorites of mine. One involves a guest who was preparing for one of the inn's famous murder mystery weekends. He came downstairs and told Sharon that he'd seen one of the actors upstairs, and commented on the authenticity of his costume. Knowing that none of the murder mystery staff were up there, she asked about the person he'd seen. "There's a gentleman upstairs with a really cool outfit, carrying a cane and wearing a top hat. I spoke to him when I passed by, and he nodded at me. He must be part of the cast of the murder mystery," the man explained. Not wanting to alarm him, she just smiled and said, "Must be," although she knew that the guest had encountered one of the inn's resident ghosts.

A couple who had visited Thayer's several times had decided that there really weren't any ghosts there, since they'd never had any experiences. On one of their stays, Sharon woke up to find that they hadn't come down to breakfast. Moreover, their room was empty — they'd apparently left abruptly without telling anyone. Since they were regular customers, Sharon assumed that they'd received an emergency call during the night or something along those lines. A few days later, the wife of the couple called her back with an explanation. As they lay in bed, they discussed the haunted reputation of the inn, and the lady said something like, "If there is a spirit here, show yourself to us!" During the night, the room got extremely cold and then suddenly as bright as if someone had turned on a huge flare. Standing at the foot of their bed, appearing slowly, was the ghost of a man. He faded away as suddenly as he came, the room became dark again, and the temperature returned to normal. It scared them so much that they left the inn.

Sharon didn't seem to be taken aback at all; as she told the woman, "Why are you surprised? It's exactly what you asked him to do!" To make a long story short, the couple continue to visit Thayer's — they are just a bit more respectful to the spirits now.

Along with the spirits of the humans that linger at the inn, there are the ghosts of a few kitties as well; cats that once belonged to Sharon — if anyone can ever truly "own" a cat, that is. Now that these felines have passed on, however, they occasionally show up at the inn. One such instance occurred when Sharon's sister was visiting Thayer's and helping out with the daily chores. There was one bed that she just couldn't straighten out — there was an indentation about the size of a cat in the middle, one that was hesitant to move.

And the ghost stories go on — pleasant things, certainly nothing scary. Molly in her blue taffeta dress, who moves things around in the rooms, the picture of Carolyn by the back door that shows her satisfaction with the current arrangement of furniture by the expression of her face, and, of course, the pennies.

Sharon has restored the inn to its original beauty and beyond, and it boasts not only antique furnishings but also romantic touches such as four-poster beds, claw-footed tubs, and even whirlpool tubs in some rooms. There are eleven bedrooms, each with its own individual personality. The beds are so comfortable that many guests come downstairs in the morning for breakfast and ask, "Where can I buy a bed like that?"

Speaking of breakfast, there is no set menu — it is decided after Sharon has had an opportunity to meet and talk with all of her guests for the evening. Special dietary considerations are taken into account, and a breakfast is prepared that will be a perfect match for everyone there. The menu always varies but is always delicious. Breakfast for the day that this chapter was written, for example, started with a fresh fruit combo, covered in a cream sauce with rosemary and sprinkled with natural brown sugar. The next course consisted of homemade orange and cranberry bagels, with all of the dressings, followed by the main course of pumpernickel bread, grilled Virginia ham, and Amish cheese with a champagne dill sauce. Dessert was a delectable offering of strawberries dipped in chocolate. Wow — I'm getting hungry just writing it all down.

Thayer's is a favorite destination for newlyweds and couples celebrating a special anniversary. Other weekends hold something for everyone, such as mother/daughter getaways, birthday teas, psychic weekend retreats, and ghost hunting packages. Or perhaps you're just looking for a restful place to leave the stress of life behind — Thayer's is the perfect destination.

There is no guarantee that you'll see the ghosts during your visit, since they usually don't bother the inn's guests. Still, they are present, watching to make sure that everything is in order, and that Thayer's continues to be "no ordinary B&B"!

Thayer's Historic Bed 'n Breakfast
60 West Elm St.
P.O. Box 246
Annandale, MN 55302
(320) 274-8222
(800) 944 6595 (reservations)
www.thayers.net

A Vacation from Ghost Hunting

Cedar Grove Inn — Vicksburg, Mississippi

WHEN MY WIFE AND I planned a vacation to Mississippi, my idea was that I'd take a break from ghost hunting and research on this book. Not that I wasn't enjoying it, but no matter what your job is, sometimes you simply have to push the chair away from the table and get up for a while.

One of our destinations was the city of Vicksburg, and when we stopped at the Tourist Bureau to get recommendations on where to eat dinner, I happened to see a brochure for the historic ghost walk. I picked it up and — well, you know what they say about the best-laid plans of mice and men. A few hours later we were bundled up, following our lantern-bearing guide through the streets of the celebrated old city, listening to wonderful tales of lingering spirits from the Civil War.

The ghost walk was presented very well, and in fact I'd have to count it among the best that I've ever been on. The guide was knowledgeable and entertaining, and provided just the right mix of hauntings and the history behind them. My ears perked up when he came to the story of Cedar Grove Inn — it turned out that I was a little familiar with the place, since we'd checked in there just a few hours before.

As the story goes, when the Union army was shelling the city of Vicksburg in 1863, only a few shots were fired at the mansion named Cedar Grove. The mistress of the house, Elizabeth Bartley Day Kline, was related to General William T. Sherman. When the Yankee soldiers found out about that, they quickly turned their cannons to other targets in the city — but not before a cannonball exploded in the house, killing Elizabeth's young son who was, ironically, named after the general. Many people in town thought that by losing a son Elizabeth had gotten what she deserved, what with her being related to not just a Yankee but a notorious officer like Sherman. Today, there are phantom footsteps on the stairways of the house as the lad continues to visit the home where he lost his mortal life.

I planned to leave the story right there — really, I did — but that just didn't work out. When we returned to our room that night, I noticed a plaque on the closet door above a gaping hole that read: *A cannonball came through this original door during the Civil War in 1863*. The house had definitely been shelled. Further exploration downstairs revealed a cannonball still lodged in one wall and a hole in the floor covered with Plexiglas where another had hit. The evidence of these artillery shells, along with the fact that the house was still standing today, gave some credence to the ghost story associated with Cedar Grove.

One thing that I've learned over the years, though, is that historical research is one of the most powerful tools in the science of ghost hunting. Whether you're conducting a detailed investigation or casually visiting a haunted location, a little digging into its past can reveal many points that might otherwise be missed. As it turned out, such was the case with Cedar Grove.

The next morning, I booked a spot for us on the tour of the inn to get a little more background on the house, then struck up a conversation with one of the staff. When I broached the subject of ghosts, her eyes darted quickly around as if she wanted to see who might be observing our conversation. It's something that I've seen before, especially in places that like to play down any aspect of the supernatural. In a low voice, she told me that there were plenty of "interesting" things that happen around the house. Since it was obvious that she was uncomfortable with the subject, I thanked her and went off to find the tour group.

The tour of the house was interesting and informative; it has a rich, old history. A young man named John Alexander Klein had built up a fortune in the city through many avenues of business. In the late 1830s, he happened to meet a young girl who was visiting in town, and was so captivated with her that he immediately planned to marry her. She was only fourteen, however, and he was forced to wait until she reached the much more mature age of sixteen years. In the meantime, he began construction on a mansion overlooking the Mississippi River for their home. Two years after the house was started, John married Elizabeth Bartley Day; she was sixteen, and he was thirty. They honeymooned in Europe for a full year, then returned to Vicksburg and Cedar Grove. The crews were still working on the house, though, so they moved into the pool house and waited for construction to be completed. It wouldn't be finished until 1852, but when it was, it was certainly a grand place.

When the War Between the States broke out, there was a scandal in town when it became known that Elizabeth was a cousin of General Sherman, and the couple experienced some social discomfort because of that fact. Cedar Grove survived the shelling of Vicksburg, and remains as one of the showplaces of the city to this day.

Our tour guide gave us that information and more, including the fact that four of the Klein's ten children had originally been buried on the grounds. Their graves were eventually moved to the city cemetery, but a marker still stands on the property. I made a mental note to check it out before leaving, then asked about the son that was named after Sherman. The guide told me that all she knew about him was that he was tragically shot at a young age, but she didn't have any more details. This was the first indication that there might be something amiss with the original ghost story. Surely if he'd been killed by shrapnel from a cannonball, it would be a tale that would be featured in the telling of any history of the house.

With a little more digging, the ghost story began to fall completely apart. While General Sherman's ties to the lady of the house may have played some part in the home being saved, there are many mansions in town that also survived: McRaven, Duff Green, and Lakemont to name but a few. In fact, the history of the Vicksburg campaign tells us that one of the major things that actually saved Cedar Grove and several of the other houses was that they were used as hospitals for both Union and Confederate soldiers after the battle had ended.

The final blow to the original story came when I visited the Klein children's marker on the grounds. There was the name "William Sherman Klein" along with the dates "born 9-23-1863, died 7-11-1879." He was born months after Vicksburg had fallen, so there is no way that his death was caused by the siege. When young William was killed by a bullet, he was nearly sixteen years old and the Civil War was long over. By checking a few sources on the history of the Klein family, it turns out that his death was due to a hunting accident, a far cry from the original tale.

I don't know who might haunt the hallways of Cedar Grove. Stories that I've uncovered since the visit include the sounds of children laughing and playing in empty halls, the smell of pipe tobacco on the main floor even though smoking isn't allowed in the house, and the ghost of a former tour guide who loved the place and said that her spirit was going to come back and visit often. If we'd stayed a few nights longer, I might have been able to befriend a staff member or two and hear their experiences or even run across one of the spirits myself. The only thing that I know for sure is that the popular ghost story about the house isn't true. Just a tiny bit of historical research — even on vacation — can prove to be a powerful tool in substantiating or debunking accounts of ghosts and hauntings.

Cedar Grove Inn
2200 Oak St.
Vicksburg, MS 39180
(800) 862-1300
(601) 636-1000
www.cedargroveinn.com

The Beer Baron's Ghost

Lemp Mansion — St. Louis, Missouri

I LOVE SURPRISES when I'm traveling. Not the kind where your flight is delayed by three hours or the hotel is overbooked and has lost your reservations; no, I'm talking about the pleasant kind.

My wife and I got a surprise like that in St. Louis recently, where we were looking for some ghostly tales and haunted places in Missouri. One of my goals in town was to find some of the best barbecue, something for which the city is known. I accomplished that task when I walked through the doors of Charlotte's Rib. It's an out-of-the-way little place, but the barbecue there was some of the best I've found. I think we brought home a case of the restaurant's homemade sauce.

My wife was looking forward to a little antiquing while we were in town, so we drove over to the epicenter of that world in St. Louis: Cherokee Street. It was a little tricky to find, but had block after block of shops with very interesting wares. Everything was there, from bargains to over-extravagant items, and we were slowly filling up our car as we worked our way up the street.

We'd been so involved in shopping that lunch quickly passed us by — when we realized that fact, we were hoping that something in the area was still open. We asked for a recommendation at the store where we happened to be shopping, and the lady behind the counter said, "Oh, you have to go to Lemp Mansion!"

So we did.

Lemp Mansion is located on DeMenil Place, which is more or less at the I-55 end of Cherokee Street. It wasn't that much of a journey at all. When we walked in and asked if they were still serving lunch, the waiter said, "For another thirty minutes, at least."

Since it was so late, we were the only ones in the restaurant and received quite a bit of personal attention. I placed my order for the Prosperity Sandwich, which was an open-face ensemble of ham, turkey, cheddar cheese sauce, bacon, and more. After the waiter took our order, he invited us to explore the mansion.

Both of us took off in different directions. It was certainly a beautiful old place, and being more or less alone, the atmosphere was peaceful and quiet. I wandered from room to room on the main floor, marveling at the craftsmanship.

When I stepped into the aviary, I felt a little pulse of energy, as if I'd stepped into some sort of electric field. I walked around the room, searching for the strongest point, and finally found it near the fountain. It was an amazing feeling — so intense that it was really an emotional moment. Not my own emotion, but something that I was picking up from whatever unseen entity was in the aviary with me.

I slowly moved around the room, feeling the ebb and flow of sensation there. I hated to move on, but since I wanted to explore the rest of the mansion, I walked past the fountain one more time, then made my way upstairs.

There are several bed and breakfast rooms on the next floor, all decorated in fine antiques. I think my favorite was the Lavender Suite, named for Lillian Handlan Lemp. Ms. Lemp was known for her elegant dresses done in that color, so much so that she was known in St. Louis society as "the Lavender Lady." It has a beautiful mantel, exquisite chandeliers, and even a fireplace in the bathroom. As I was looking out of the window at the view of St. Louis, my wife walked in and said, "Did you go into the room downstairs with the plants painted on the walls? Something *very* strong is in there." She had experienced the same thing that I did. We quickly looked around upstairs, then went back to the aviary just to see if the spirit was still present — it was, and continued to be a very strong, emotional force.

We heard the waiter in the next room bringing out our lunch, so we reluctantly left the aviary and sat down to a delicious meal.

I do have to give a hearty recommendation for the Prosperity Sandwich — not only was it delicious, but it was a formidable meal. As we dined, my wife and I talked about the wonderful old house and the things we'd seen on our individual excursions. At one point, as she was describing the ladies' restroom, we had to stop eating so that she could take me there to show me the shower that stood in the middle of the room. It was certainly an extravagant mansion. As we came to find out, it was built in the 1860s and was the home of William J. Lemp. The Lemp name was very prestigious in St. Louis and had its roots in the beer brewing business.

William's father, John Adam Lemp, had been a grocer in St. Louis who sold a lager beer that he brewed from an old family recipe. The beer soon began to outsell anything else at the store, so John closed his grocery and opened a full-time brewery in 1840. The business exploded into producing the most popular beer in the city, and by the 1860s it passed to John's son, William J. Lemp. He built a new, larger brewery and purchased the house that would become known as Lemp Mansion.

By 1870, the brewery had the largest share of the regional beer market. The Lemp fortune continued to grow, and William and his wife were the height of St. Louis society. In 1897 there was a wedding of royal proportions when the Lemps' daughter, Hilda, was joined in marriage to Gustav Pabst, from the famous Pabst brewing family. Life was good.

William brought up his favorite son, Frederick, in the business, teaching him all the tricks and trade of brewing in preparation for the day that the young man would take over the family business. That day would never come, however. The pressure of the business was too great, and Frederick died of a heart attack in 1901. William was distraught, and slowly began to become a recluse. His depression deepened, and in 1904 he committed suicide by gunshot in his bedroom at Lemp Mansion.

William J. Lemp, Jr. took over the family business upon the death of his father, and he and his wife, "the Lavender Lady," spent money lavishly. Prohibition was enacted in 1919, and the family's fortunes suddenly crumbled. After selling the brewery to the International Shoe Company, William Lemp, Jr. committed suicide in his office at Lemp Mansion.

Tragedy haunted the Lemp family. Charles Lemp, another brother and the only family member left occupying the house, began to spiral down into a world of germ phobia and seclusion. In 1949, he led his dog down to the basement. Charles took his pet's life, then his own, completing the trilogy of suicides that occurred at Lemp Mansion.

The house passed from the Lemp family and changed owners several times. For a while, it was even a boarding house. In 1975, it was purchased by the Pointer family who gave it the tender loving care that it needed. During the restoration period, workers reported many strange things: knockings, phantom footsteps, and other unexplainable sounds. When the Lemp Mansion was opened as a bed and breakfast/restaurant, the staff and patrons alike began to have supernatural experiences. The strange sounds continued, along with the sounds of music from a piano that no one was playing and doors opening and closing, locking and unlocking. A female ghost was occasionally seen, thought to be that of Lillian Handlan Lemp, the "Lavender Lady."

We don't know who the mysterious spirit was that greeted us in the aviary, but the presence was strong and memorable. And so was the Lemp Mansion. We'll be back to stay in the bed and breakfast, but also for another meal. That Prosperity Sandwich was delicious, and I'm looking forward to enjoying another one.

Lemp Mansion Restaurant & Inn
3322 DeMenil Place
St. Louis, MO 63118
(314) 664-8024
www.lempmansion.com

The Temperance Ghost

Chico Hot Springs Lodge & Ranch, Montana

THE HEALING POWER of natural spring water has always fascinated me. From the natural baths of Hot Springs, Arkansas, to the Fountain of Youth in St. Augustine, Florida, the stories never fail to catch my interest. There was a time in America when people believed that drinking or bathing in certain natural spring waters could heal everything from horrible diseases to the discomforts of age — something that the medical world of today dismisses categorically.

Now, while I don't necessarily disagree with current medicinal knowledge, I also don't like to throw out all of the old-school methods either. With that in mind, you'll sometimes find me staying at one of the old mineral water hotels when I travel, just to soak up the ambiance of the old resorts, and maybe take a dip in the healing waters — just in case there is something to the stories.

If I can find one of these places with a ghost story or two, well, that's hitting a home run. I always keep my eyes open for something like that.

While we were traveling through the northern United States, we stopped by the mother of all hot springs: Yellowstone

National Park. Those certainly aren't the kind of waters that you'd want to bathe in; a dip of your big toe in those crystal clear pools would sear it right off. While we were visiting the park, however, I heard about a place a little north of there, in Montana to be exact, which not only had healing springs but also a fascinating ghost story. It also boasted activities from horseback riding to dog-sledding — my kind of place!

The springs at Chico were first discovered by Indians, who held a reverence for such places. Bathing in the springs was often part of cleansing and healing ceremonies. The first Anglo settlers who moved in were miners in search of metals ranging from precious gold to practical copper. The miners would stop at the hot springs to bathe in the warm, 112 degree water — it was the only way they could get a hot bath without having to boil gallons of water first. While they were there, they would wash out all of their clothes and blankets, taking full advantage of the luxury afforded with the springs.

The name for the hot springs dated way back to 1868, when a mail route was established through that part of Montana. One of the miners who had frequented the area was nicknamed "Chico," and he was very popular with the other miners. He entertained them with his jokes and stories, and made the harsh life of the others a little easier. Chico moved on, but his friends remembered him. When it came time to assign a name, they decided on "Chico Hot Springs."

Campers were constantly at the hot springs, a fact that didn't escape the notice of several entrepreneurs. There were many plans to build hotels, spas, resorts, and more — by the late 1800s, however, none of these elaborate plans had materialized. But folks still flocked to the hot water.

Bill and Percie Knowles took over the property in 1894. Although there was no palatial resort there, they opened a boarding house for miners who were working in the area or just passing through in search of a mother lode farther north or to the west. A steady business provided the capital that they needed, and just a few years later on June 20, 1900, the hotel was complete. It was built at the base of the majestic Emigrant Peak, a volcano that was active during the Eocene period, thirty-five million to fifty-five million years ago.

The Knowleses were very good at marketing their hotel. They enlisted drivers to bring guests from the Emigrant Peak train depot directly to the resort, making it an attractive vacation destination. Bill decided to take entertainment there to the next level by opening a dance hall and a bar — kind of a discotheque for the times. Percie was categorically against it, since she was a teetotaling temperance lady.

Whether Bill brought his destiny on himself in some self-fulfilling prophesy of Percie's or a cruel twist of fate intervened, Bill fell ill with cirrhosis of the liver and died on April 22, 1910.

Percie was distraught at the loss of her husband, but was even more resolved against the demon alcohol. With the help of their son, Radbourne, she turned the hotel into a hospital that provided treatment using the healing hot springs. She was able to attract Dr. George Townsend to be a physician in residence, adding credibility to the hospital and attracting patients from across the nation.

After more than a decade of service to the hospital, the good doctor retired. While many capable physicians followed him, the reputation of the place was never the same. Fewer and fewer people came for treatment, and Chico Hot Springs began to decline.

Much as the fictional story of Dorian Gray, Percie Knowles' health went down with the decline of her hospital. Her mental faculties began to fail her, and she spent the last years of her life in her room, sitting in her rocking chair and staring into oblivion.

She was finally committed to the state institution where she passed away in 1940.

Ownership of the hospital-hotel passed to her son, who followed her in death just a few years later. Following that, several owners tried to resurrect the old place — some kept the health theme, others went the hotel route, and one even tried to introduce gambling on the premises. None were successful, until a couple from Ohio purchased it in 1973 and transformed it into the beautiful resort that it is today.

You will find Chico Hot Springs listed on the National Register of Historic Places. It is also recognized as a perfect example of the mineral spring resorts of the age. And while a visitor can also take in wonderful experiences such as rafting, hiking, fishing, or skiing, there's something else that you might encounter during your stay there: a visit from Bill or Percie, who still seem to be checking in on their hotel.

The most active spirit seems to be that of Percie, who has been seen as a female figure in a white dress wafting through the hallways. Her activity is intensified in Rooms 346 to 350, an area that encompasses her personal room in the last years of her life.

The staff has also been alerted to the clanking and clattering of pots and pans in the kitchen after it has been closed down and locked up, as if someone was in there rearranging things — something that Percie might be doing just to get everything set up as she pleases.

One of the most interesting things about the hotel is that the ghost stories don't only come from the guests but also from the security guards and other employees that work there. Whatever is going on at Chico Hot Springs Resort and Day Spa, however benevolent, it seems to be very active. Perhaps Percie is returning to frown upon any drinking at her hospital, or maybe Bill is returning to liven up the party a little bit.

Whatever the case, you're going to have a great time at Chico Hot Springs. There are year-round activities to make your stay memorable. In fact, I defy you to find a resort that has so many activities that you can come back time after time and still not cover them all. Put this place on your calendar, and get ready for some dog-sledding, skiing, rafting, plus all the luxuries of a spa. All that, and if you're lucky, you might just run into Percie as well... and if you do, it's probably best not to offer her a glass of wine!

Chico Hot Springs Resort and Day Spa
1 Chico Road
Pray, MT 59065
(800) HOT-WADA
(406) 333-4933
www.chicohotsprings.com

The Speakeasy Spirits

The Argo Hotel — Crofton, Nebraska

HISTORIC OLD HOTELS have a lifetime of stories to tell — usually several in fact. It's common for such buildings to have served in many capacities over the years. That usually makes for colorful stories about their pasts, and often can explain some of the strange goings-on that are noticed when the doors are locked and the lights are extinguished. Such a places is the Argo Hotel in the charming city of Crofton, up in the northeast corner of the Cornhusker State — Nebraska.

Today there are almost a thousand people in Crofton, but the roots of the people there go back thousands of years. In fact, some of the human remains found in the area date back to over a thousand years B.C. In the more recent times, during the Plains period (1600 to 1800) it is estimated that around forty thousand Indians lived in the state, including Sioux, Cheyenne, Omaha, Pawnee, Arapaho, and many others.

The first Europeans that came to Nebraska were fur traders from France who arrived in the late 1600s. They began to trade with the Indians, and settlements soon began to dot the wilderness. Lewis and Clark came through the area in 1804; in fact, it took them five days to cross the Missouri River just north of

Crofton. The Mormons came through some forty-odd years later, wintering near Crofton before continuing their journey. The territory of Nebraska was created in 1865, which led to the first formal settlements. In 1892, the city of Crofton was established. While the region was once occupied by trappers, farmers soon realized the value of the land and made up the initial population of the town. To name the town, suggestions were written on slips of paper and drawn out one by one. Each name was discussed, and dismissed if anyone had a strong objection. Someone had submitted the name Crofton after the community of Crofton Courts in England, and since no one could think of a reason against it, the name passed the vote.

The first two buildings in town were reportedly saloons, built across the street from each other — apparently the settlers wanted a place or two to kick up their heels a little. As the town grew, other buildings were added: stores, a bank, a school, and a lumberyard to supply the ever-growing town with building supplies. People continued to move to town, and as recorded in the history of the Argo Hotel, by 1912 the town contained over forty businesses, a booming four lumberyards, a railroad that boasted five trains through town ever day, and over a hundred working girls, or "ladies of the evening."

A Greek immigrant named Nick Michaelis watched the parade of visitors coming to town, and envisioned a grand hotel to house them during their stay. He approached the city fathers with the idea and struck a deal with them: If the city would install a sewer system, he would build the hotel.

Build it he did, and it became a grand showplace, easily the finest hotel in the region. Nick gave it the name of the ship that brought him from Greece to America, the Argo. That ship was named after the famous vessel in the Greek tale of Jason and the Argonauts, which in turn was named for Argus, the famed shipbuilder.

The Argo Hotel operated as a luxurious inn until 1940, when it took on a completely different life: that of a natural healing center. It wasn't a classic hospital with an emergency room or operating theater. Instead it boasted specialty treatments for those who were chronically or severely ill — people who had not found success with standard medical practices. The center had any number of therapies available to the patients there: mud baths, customized potions, massage therapy, and many other radical treatments. One of the first x-ray machines in the nation was located at the center as well. A staff of forty doctors made sure that every patient received personalized care and attention. It wasn't long before there were stories of miraculous cures and spontaneous healing spreading from the clinic throughout the territory.

There were some problems, however. Of the staff of forty doctors, not a single one was a licensed physician, and their brand of treatment amounted to more or less guesswork. Some patients were able to recover from their illnesses at the clinic, probably just from the rest that they got. Others, though, fell victim to their diseases and died at the clinic. This was one of the darker chapters in the history of the building. Those who were dying were often relegated to the basement so that no one would observe their terminal condition. When they passed on, their bodies were secreted out the back door in the dead of night so as not to hurt the clinic's reputation. If anyone asked about the missing patients, tales were invented about their wonderful cures.

Eventually the truth about the clinic came out, the doors were closed, and the building was abandoned. Horrible stories continued to circulate about the place, however, giving it an air of mystery and foreboding. It sat empty for years.

In 1994 the Argo Hotel was purchased by new owners, and a renovation process was launched to restore it to its original beauty. Many parts of the hotel were gutted and rebuilt, and you're going to love the results. From the plush, burgundy accents to the dark wood trim, it would make ol' Nick Michaelis proud.

Some reminders of its colorful past continue to be present at the Argo, however. Some say that the spirits of those who died here, those whose deaths were quieted as the bodies were slipped away into the night, continue to walk the halls. The most active part of the hotel is — you guessed it — the basement where so many were taken to die in silence.

Today, the basement has been renamed the Garden Level and is the location of the hotel's nightclub, the Speak Easy. The lounge contains a one hundred year old bar, fireplaces, and a cigar room for those who want to enjoy a good stogie.

Employees are sometimes afraid to descend the staircase alone, because they often have the feeling that someone is watching them as they go about their business in the bar. This was especially true during the renovation process, when workmen reported that they dreaded working in the basement, since an unseen presence seemed to be down there with them.

A cool breeze has been felt in the hotel, even when the air is warm and still outside. Shadows are also seen walking through the hallway, stepping into doorways or around corners just as someone catches a glimpse of them.

Who are these spirits? Well, some feel they are some of the folks who died there many years ago. Since their death was ignored back then — hushed up even — it's possible that they are returning just so the people of today will remember how they lost their lives so many years ago.

Don't fret, though, the spirits of the Argo are friendly; they just like to hang out in the Speak Easy lounge. In a beautifully restored, historic old hotel like the Argo, who can blame them?

The Argo Hotel
211 Kansas St.
Crofton, NE 68730
(402) 388-2400
(800) 607-ARGO
www.theargohotel.com

What Happens in Vegas, Stays in Vegas

•●●●•

Luxor Hotel and Casino — Las Vegas, Nevada

WE'D TRAVELED FROM AFAR, crossing the sands toward our destination. It was a legendary place where we hoped to discover wealth and prosperity, a place where untold riches awaited the traveler with fortune on his side. Finally, we were able to see it in the distance: the peak of the pyramid rising up from the desert. Its very sight made us move faster, and soon we could see the familiar, mystic figure of the sphinx standing a watchful guard, along with a tall obelisk emblazoned with hieroglyphics.

How did the ancient Egyptians align the pyramids so that two sides ran so precisely on a north-south axis? That is only one of the mysteries that surround those faraway structures. The Great Pyramids of Egypt have been a source of mystery for many years. Of course, they were built as tombs to the great pharaohs, but they were much more than that. The pyramids were believed to possess some kind of supernatural powers that would help to lead the rulers into the afterlife. Today, there are those who believe that pyramids continue to display powers far beyond the understanding of present-day culture.

We weren't on the Giza Plateau for our trip, however — we weren't even standing on the ancient sands of Egypt. Instead, my wife and I had made our way to that city of sin and neon: Las Vegas, Nevada. At the southern end of the world-famous Las Vegas Strip is a huge pyramid that is majestically guarded by a sphinx.

The Luxor hotel and casino is a marvel of modern engineering. The hotel's rooms are located along the angled walls of the hotel, and each hallway looks down into the interior of the pyramid. In each corner is an elevator designed especially for the Luxor that goes up at the angle of the pyramid. They have been dubbed "inclinators," since they take passengers on an incline instead of straight up.

Getting back to the Luxor's Egyptian counterparts, when archeologists were examining the inner chambers of the pyramids, they found that stray cats that had become lost in the tombs when they were sealed had mysteriously become perfectly mummified over the years.

Because of that, a French explorer named Monsieur Bovis went home and constructed a precise, scaled-down model of the pyramid. When he placed a dead cat in his model, it mummified perfectly. Further experiments over the years found that razor blades placed inside a pyramid retained sharpness much longer than normal. It was also found to keep food fresher, tenderized meat, and aided in reducing headache pain — and possibly increased sexual ability. Some even believe that a pyramid somehow causes polarized microwave signals that could eventually be channeled in a form of electrical power!

So what does all this have to do with a hotel and casino in Las Vegas? Well, your guess is as good as anyone else's. There is one thing for certain: Guests have reported seeing the misty forms of a spirit roaming the hallways of the hotel.

The question begs to be asked, of course, as to how such a relatively new location could be haunted. I suppose that it could be the spirit of one or more of the three people who have taken their own life at the hotel, throwing themselves over the railing of one of the higher floors. On the other hand, the haunting could be related to the two workmen who reportedly lost their lives in accidents during the construction of the hotel. Many histories of Vegas state that "there are many holes in the desert," referring to the time when the city was ruled by mobsters and impromptu executions and burials took place away from the major hotels — the Luxor property is at the far south end of the strip, where nothing stood in the old days, and could easily be the location of such activity. Spirits of any gangsters could be responsible for the apparitions seen in the hotel. Or maybe it is the power of the pyramid alone that attracts the specters. Whatever the case, something supernatural seems to be happening at the Luxor.

It is not only interesting from that perspective but also from its design. The pyramid reaches three hundred fifty feet (146.73 meters) into the sky and is thirty-six stories tall. Luxor is home to the world's largest atrium, measuring twenty-nine million cubic feet. The hotel has four thousand four hundred seven rooms, making it the third largest hotel in the world. The beam crowning the pyramid is the brightest beam in the world, and is comprised of forty-five Xenon lights. It is said that you can read a newspaper ten miles in space by its light. Combine all that with the detailed Egyptian theme and the hospitality of the staff, and you have a wonderful place to stay in Las Vegas. And who knows — you might even run into a spirit or two. If you do, though, don't worry. Like the saying goes about the city, "What happens in Vegas, stays in Vegas!"

Luxor Hotel and Casino
3900 Las Vegas Blvd. South
Las Vegas, NV 89119-1000
(702) 262-4444
(800) 288-1000
www.luxor.com

Spirits of the New England Shakers

✶ • ● ● • ✶

The Shaker Inn — Enfield, New Hampshire

THE NAME OF this religion comes from the practice of violent trembling, spinning, and dancing during the worship services of the Shaker people. They had their beginnings around 1750 in Manchester, England, as an offshoot of the Quaker faith. They were often referred to as "shaking Quakers," or simply "Shakers."

An early leader of the church was Ann Lee, who believed that she was being shown visions from God. These revelations included the fact that sex should be avoided, because it was the root of all sin; that she had been chosen by God to spread the faith to the New World; and, as if that wasn't already enough, that she was the embodiment of the second coming of Christ.

The Quaker religion believed that the second coming of the Lord would be in the form of a woman, so the fact that a strong, charismatic woman like Mother Ann (as she became known) surfaced in their church was thought to be a divine sign. At the very least, they regarded her as a prophet.

Ann did go to America, and other Shaker groups soon followed. One such congregation settled in New Hampshire in the late 1700s, and by 1837 a four-year construction project had begun on what the group called the "Great Stone Dwelling."

Made of granite and six stories high, it was the largest Quaker dwelling in the world, and was built to be its own, self-contained community. The first floor contained the kitchen and the dining hall, along with the retiring rooms, which were used for sleeping and for studying religious materials before or after meals. The second floor contained the Great Meeting Hall, a room large enough to hold two hundred people and easily accommodate the religious practices of the group, which included precision dances and marches. Services also included other rituals such as shouting, speaking in unknown tongues, healing, pronouncing prophecy, visions, and spirit-induced trances. The upper floors contained living quarters that were divided into the "Brothers' Side" and the "Sisters' Side," since mingling between the sexes was strictly forbidden.

For many members of the Enfield Shaker congregation, the Great Stone Dwelling became their entire world. In fact, contact with outsiders, those called "The World's People," was forbidden. Because some interaction was required, however, one man was appointed as the liaison between the Enfield Shakers and the neighboring communities. That man's name was Caleb Dyer.

Caleb walked a fine line between keeping to his Shaker beliefs and dealing with the outside world, but he became very successful in the role. The congregation came to depend on his business savvy and levelheaded abilities.

In 1863 a man approached Caleb for a favor. He was heading off to enlist as a Union soldier but had two daughters in his care. He asked Caleb if the Shaker community would take them in and keep them safe. The girls were welcomed, and the man marched off to war.

Six months later, the father reappeared at the door of the Great Stone Dwelling to demand his daughters back. He was very gruff and obviously inebriated. Caleb came out to try to reason with him, and was understandably reluctant to turn the two young girls over to their father.

The more insistent he became, the more resolve Caleb showed. The Shaker leader was convinced that given the father's current condition, the girls would be much better off with the congregation. As the argument heated up, the father produced a gun and shot Caleb dead.

The Enfield Shakers had a tough time without Caleb and his business knowledge, and suffered greatly at the loss. Their numbers dwindled off; since sexual relations were forbidden, no children were produced, and the congregation had to depend solely on converts to continue to exist and grow.

The Great Stone Dwelling finally found its new purpose as an inn that is elegant in its simplicity. Its earmark of "Fine Dining and Historic Lodging" rings true, since the twenty-four guest rooms are faithfully restored with Shaker furniture. You will find the inn, which is situated on the peaceful shores of Lake Mascoma, to be a wonderfully relaxing place to spend a few days. You'll marvel at the access that you have to the structure and at the furnishings that are beautiful in their simplicity.

You may also discover one of the Shaker Inn's secrets: Some of its former inhabitants sometimes return to visit the stone building that was once their home. Guests at the inn have reported the sound of doors opening and closing on floors where no one is staying. There are also footsteps in the inn that cannot be attributed to any human being there — the phenomenon takes place in empty hallways, unoccupied rooms, and on upstairs floors that are still being restored.

Room 15 has a particularly interesting presence. The staff has come into the room on several occasions to see a rocking chair there gently moving back and forth, as if some unseen Shaker from many years ago is relaxing there.

Legend also has it that one of the innkeepers had shut down the Shaker Inn one evening, turning off all the lights and locking the door since there were no guests present. As he drove away, he glanced back and saw that the kitchen lights had been turned on. He turned his car around, returned to the inn, and discovered that some unseen hand had flipped on the switches. As he explored the kitchen, he felt the brush of a presence pass by him — another Shaker who has returned to visit the granite fortress that was once home.

The Enfield Shaker Inn
24 Caleb Dyer Lane
Enfield, NH 03748
(603) 632-4900
www.theshakerinn.com

A Series of Strange Occurrences

Jimmy's Haunt — Morristown, New Jersey

 ONE RULE OF THUMB that I used when visiting places for this book was that the establishment had to have publicly talked about its haunts before — I'm not in the business of "outing" any haunted locations. Imagine my surprise when, in New Jersey, I found a place that actually incorporated its ghostly reputation into its name! Jimmy's Haunt is such a place — it's located in Morristown, and openly advertises that there is a supernatural side to the restaurant.

First of all, this is one of those places that I'd be happy to visit whether it had ghosts or not. When you sit down and start perusing the menu, your mouth is going to start watering immediately. Start out with some Grilled Lobster Skewers, and as you're nibbling on them, sit back and just try to make a decision on your entrée — go ahead, I dare you. You can dine on Lemon Chicken and Penne Pasta, Oriental Barbecued Duck Breast, Maryland Jumbo Crab Cakes, or Grilled Shrimp in Red Thai Curry. Man, that all sounds good. For me, though, the choice comes down to one menu item: the Seared Filet Mignon.

As if that weren't enough food, you can crown your meal with a scrumptious desert, with goodies ranging from apple pie to cheesecake to chocolate fondue. Ahhhh... let me just sit at the table and digest a while. Outstanding.

I almost forgot that I was writing about ghosts at Jimmy's Haunt. Almost, that is. Once I started digging into its history, I was able to forget about the delicious food — at least for a few minutes.

Morristown, New Jersey, collected a number of historical footnotes during the 1700s. Originally, it was a stagecoach stop on the route through New Jersey. George Washington wintered his command nearby because of the nearby powder mill and iron-works. The building that is now Jimmy's Haunt was constructed in the mid-1700s, 1749 to be exact, by a man named John Sayre.

American statesman Alexander Hamilton proposed marriage to his fiancée Elizabeth Schuyler in the taproom of the pub. They were married in 1780, and during the course of their lives had eight children together.

By the early 1800s, the place had passed from John Sayre to Judge Samuel Sayre and his wife, Sarah. On May 11, 1833, something terrible happened there — it would only be discussed in whispers for years afterward, and its ramifications may still be felt today.

Judge Samuel lived at the house with his wife and their live-in maid, Phoebe. They took in another boarder, a hired hand, to help with some of the heavier work around the house. His name was Antoine Le Blanc, and he had come to America from France to establish a home before sending for his fiancée, a girl named Marie Smicht who lived in Germany. While Mr. Le Blanc was a respected young man back in France, he brokered a less-than-desirable deal for himself at the Sayre household. He was to do upkeep, repair, and any other handyman jobs, and in return he would receive room and board — but no monetary compensation. After a short while of chopping wood and slopping the hogs, he became disillusioned with the arrangement, even angry. While he had been a well-to-do man, he was now little more than an indentured servant. Even Phoebe the maid ordered him around.

Finally, in the confines of his small basement apartment, he snapped. After drinking at a local pub one evening, he returned to the Sayre home with a vicious hate in his heart.

Antoine killed the judge and then his wife by beating them mercilessly with a shovel. The crime scene was grisly beyond description — he continued until their faces were almost unrecognizable. He then went to the maid's bedroom and caved in Phoebe's skull with a single blow from a club. After taking a number of valuables from the house, he ran away into the night.

The next morning a neighbor made the terrible discovery, and the local police found a trail of the Sayres' belongings that led them to Le Blanc, who was at a pub in a neighboring town. It was a horrific crime, one that shocked the people of Morristown.

Antoine Le Blanc was immediately arrested and was put on trial for the murders in three months' time. The attorney handling the defense asked for a change of venue, but the court was reportedly swayed by the massive anger of the local citizens and refused to move the trial. Le Blanc never confessed, and after both sides argued their cases, the jury of local citizens found him guilty after only twenty minutes of deliberation. The presiding judge, the Honorable Gabriel Ford, directed that he "be hanged by the neck until dead" and then "be delivered to Dr. Isaac Canfield, a surgeon, for dissection."

But the story doesn't end there. It takes a very macabre turn. On September 6, Antoine was led to a gallows built on the town green, where approximately ten thousand people had gathered to watch him die. One thing to note is that the city of Morristown had a population of a little less than three thousand people at the time, so the event had drawn quite a large crowd.

When the executioner threw the wooden switch, a counterweight dropped and Le Blanc was jerked eight feet into the air. His body twitched and, after a couple of minutes, became still.

His body was hurriedly cut down and taken back to the courtroom, where two doctors were waiting on it.

Next, a series of experiments was conducted on the corpse. The doctors were researching a Frankenstein-like theory that electrical currents controlled the body and could do so even after death. They ran electricity through Le Blanc's body, and while they were unsuccessful at reviving it, they did make some muscles twitch.

Afterward, the doctors peeled the skin off of the body, and it was taken to a tanner to be preserved. Soon, residents of the city could purchase a piece of Antoine Le Blanc, autographed by the local sheriff for authenticity. Larger pieces of skin were made into wallets, book covers, and other items — it sounds like something out of a horror movie instead of the dispensing of New England justice, but it actually happened.

The Sayres' house was eventually sold, even though the memory of the murders was still very fresh in the minds of the local people. Alderman James Lidgerwood purchased the property and held many social events there. I doubt that his guests were ever truly comfortable, though. It was during the Lidgerwood era that another tragedy took place at the house. One of its inhabitants committed suicide but left no clue as to what had led to such an act — even to this day there is no explanation.

The property changed hands once again in 1946, when Edward Winchester bought it to open a restaurant there — Winchester's Turnpike Inn. Eleven years later, on October 25, 1957, a fire spread quickly through the restaurant. Workers tried to call the fire department, but mysteriously enough the telephones would not work, even though the flames were nowhere near the switch in the restaurant. Help was finally summoned from a nearby call box, and by the time the fire was extinguished twenty-five men had been injured in the process.

The restaurant was purchased again in 1960 by William McClausand and reopened as the Wedgewood Inn. A problem quickly arose, however, because no matter what the management tried, there was no way to control the temperature in Phoebe's room. No matter what time of year it was, there was an otherworldly chill there. Candles that had been lit in the room, once extinguished, would light again. The electrical lights would flip on or off, and visitors to the room described a feeling that they were not alone.

The building changed hands many times over the next few decades; in 1981, it was opened as a club named Society Hill. Phoebe's spirit continued to be active from the very first day, and in fact, there were any number of problems that occurred when the grand opening was set — unknowingly — on the anniversary of the Sayre murders. When the newly named restaurant did open, the party was interrupted when a punchbowl filled with refreshments for the guests exploded on its own.

The building has endured many incarnations, including Argyle's All-American, South Street, and, perhaps in an effort to appease the active spirit there, even Phoebe's Restaurant.

Today, the legend of Antoine Le Blanc is closely entwined with the structure. In fact, the most prominent supernatural activities are still attributed to the murdered maid, Phoebe.

Her spirit is said to open and close doors, always catching the restaurant staff by surprise. A cool, gentle breeze wafting up the stairs to the room where Phoebe died has been noticed for years and years. Lights that are on get suddenly switched off, and dark rooms are suddenly illuminated by light, even though no one is present there.

Something in the basement of the restaurant seems to creep out the staff, because when the place is dark and quiet, no one seems to want to go down there alone.

You may go to Jimmy's in search of a supernatural experience, but I promise you that the menu will soon become your primary focus. They do a wonderful job there — I'm sure that even Phoebe agrees.

Jimmy's Haunt
217 South St.
Morristown, NJ 07960-5336
(973) 455-7000
www.jimmyshaunt.com

A New Mexico Dynasty

Luna Mansion — Los Lunas, New Mexico

AS I WAS WORKING on this chapter, we were traveling to the southwestern part of the country in search of good food, interesting places, the beauty of the desert, and a ghost story or two along the way. I knew of several haunted places in Albuquerque, but a friend gave me a sterling piece of advice: For some very interesting haunts, head south to the city of Los Lunas.

We did just that, and were thrilled with what we found. Not only did we have a first-class meal, but we found a place steeped in history: the Luna Mansion. Its past alone makes for wonderful reading — it could almost be a television show. Too bad the name *Dynasty* has already been used!

The story begins back in the late 1600s, almost at the turn of the century, when the king of Spain controlled New Mexico. The king gave a land grant to a gentleman named Domingo de Luna, and he soon built a fortune in livestock. As fate would have it, the king of Spain granted land to another baron, Don Pedro Otero, in a neighboring county.

Each of the two men headed families that became rich and powerful. Their descendants grew in society and in politics, and since their paths began to cross, the two clans became powerful friends. The families entered into business together, and in a dual Romeo and Juliet story, children from both sides fell in love. In the late 1800s, Solomon Luna married Adelaida Otero, and Manuel Otero married Eloisa Luna. The Luna-Otero dynasty had ascended to power in the territory. Sounding interesting so far? You bet — as I was digging through the history of the Luna family, I honestly felt like I was reading some fascinating fictional script.

It gets better.

In 1880, as the Santa Fe Railroad was planning its trek through the territory, it laid one track across Luna property. Actually, the train tracks would bisect the family home. As part of the deal that was negotiated, the railroad would finance and build a new hacienda. The head of the family at the time, Don Antonio Jose Luna, was given free reign to design a new house for his family.

As a prominent family they had traveled extensively throughout the south, which contributed to the southern colonial exterior of the new mansion's design. The Spanish influence is shown in the overall adobe construction of the house.

Don Antonia died before he could move into the new family home, and for years it was passed along to various family members. The mansion experienced a revival during the 1920s, when the mistress of the house was Josefita Manderfield Otero, wife of the current head of the family, Don Eduardo.

Josefita oversaw the construction of the solarium, the front portico, the ironwork around the property, and other fineries of the mansion. Josefita, who was affectionately known as "Pepe" to her friends and family, also had an artistic flair. She painted the murals in the house and many of the paintings that hang in the mansion today. Many people credit Pepe for being the heart and soul of Luna Mansion — and many say that she still returns to visit the home that she loved so much.

When we arrived for dinner, we were told that there would be a short wait, but that we could go upstairs to the lounge for a drink. We did just that, and climbed the majestic staircase to the second floor. At the top was a beautifully carved wooden rocker, sitting there as if its last occupant had been staring down the stairs to watch people as they came from the first floor. From there, we walked the hardwood floors to the upstairs lounge. To our surprise, the lounge wasn't packed with typical bar tables and chairs — instead, it had plush furniture with an inviting atmosphere. We took a seat with our friends, ordered a frosty beverage, and started up a conversation with the bartender. When I told him that we were waiting for a table downstairs because we wanted to sit in the area where the spirits had been seen, he just laughed.

"You're in the right place," he said with a smile. "Josefita loves to hang out up here." He proceeded to tell us how, just a few nights ago, he'd been closing up and saw a woman sitting at one of the tables at the far side of the room. He'd already started turning off lights, so he couldn't see her that clearly, only that she was wearing a light-colored dress. When he apologized for starting to close down while she was still there, she only smiled. He turned the lights back on, only to find that he was alone on the floor, even though no one would have had time to get out of the room.

That was enough for us — we decided to eat right there, and just see if we were joined by any of the mansion's ghosts for the meal. The food was delicious. The restaurant features prime rib, steak, seafood, New Mexican dishes, home-style meals, and many other mouth-watering delights.

Although we didn't get to see Josefita during our dinner, I took the opportunity to go downstairs and have a conversation with the owner/manager of the property. He was a very friendly gentleman, and shared many of his ghost stories with me.

One of his most memorable stories was about being alone in the restaurant, locking everything down for the evening. While making his rounds upstairs, he noticed the fringe on a lamp moving. Thinking that someone had left an air conditioner blowing, he went to turn it off — only to find that it was not on. Looking back at the lamp, he could now see that it was moving as if someone's finger was gently brushing along it. It was then that he saw the form of Josefita appear, dressed in white, her hair put up in a bun.

I was very intrigued, so I asked if that was the last time he'd seen her. "No," he said kind of thoughtfully, "she walked across the downstairs dining room — was it last night? Or the night before?"

I was amazed that such a dramatic supernatural event was something so nonchalant to him, but then again, apparently Josefita makes herself home there at Luna Mansion, even after passing on to the other side.

He has seen her staring out of a second floor window as he was walking outside one evening, and has even had guests relate the same experience.

The fact that Josefita is present isn't always indicated by someone seeing her form, however. Sometimes the staff and guests feel extreme cold spots in the mansion, while on other occasions they've heard voices calling their names. Josefita also occasionally unscrews the light bulbs on some of the chandeliers. The owner said that on one very active evening, she was pulling the hair of one of the guests in the dining room, and then proceeded to pop all of the light bulbs in the chandelier above their table — shards of glass were falling down everywhere. He calmly told them the story of Josefita, then offered to replace their dinners. To his amazement, they actually stayed. The staff brought out a ladder and replaced the bulbs, and the meal continued in peace. I guess that Josefita had made her presence known, and was satisfied with that.

I'd like to say that we encountered the lovely Josefita that evening, but she was quiet while we were there. Perhaps she knew that we were believers and didn't feel the need to show up. Or maybe she was simply in another part of the mansion; whatever the case, the prestigious lady of Luna Mansion was otherwise occupied during our visit.

We did enjoy a wonderful meal there, along with a dessert menu that I'm sure added half an inch to my waistline — but Lord, was it delicious. As we were dining, the owner made his way upstairs and visited with us awhile, telling us more stories about the haunts at the restaurant. In the course of things, I commented about the chair at the top of the stairs. He just grinned and told me to keep an eye on it while I was in the restaurant, since Josefita seemed to like the top landing of the staircase quite a bit. Even after we paid the bill and began to leave, I kept my eye trained on it, hoping that we'd see it start to slowly move back and forth with a gentle motion as the lady of the house rested there for the evening.

Luna Mansion
110 West Main
Los Lunas, NM 87031
(505) 865-7333

The Speakeasy Spirits

Chumley's — New York, New York

NEW YORK — The Big Apple. Gotham. Capital of the World. The City that Never Sleeps. The City So Nice They Named It Twice. There are more names for this place than you can possibly imagine, and it has just as many interesting sites to visit.

As I began to comb the city for ghost stories, I found a plethora of them just waiting for a writer to choose. Some of the most interesting stories that I found didn't have anything to do with ghosts, so while I couldn't dedicate a chapter in this book to them, I couldn't help but stop and listen.

For example, when I asked about ghost stories, I was told about this strange phenomena associated with the Empire State Building. "These tourists, they get up on top, and toss off a penny for good luck. They don't mean anything bad, but those little copper discs begin to pick up speed and accelerate like a bullet. Fortunately, most of them land flat side first and just bounce around for a second. The ones that land edge-first, though, embed themselves in the concrete — you can see them all around the building. There have been a few gruesome cases as well, where some unlucky pedestrian was walking along and one hit him edge first in the top of the head. It buries itself deep inside the brain, causing that poor soul to fall over like a sack of soft potatoes. The first few times it happened, the police were mystified — a little bloody slit at the top of the head was all they found on the victim. Once they realized what was going on, they always took a good first look at the head if they found someone sprawled out on the pavement below the Empire State Building."

Interesting story, isn't it? Kind of made me want to open a hardhat concession at the base of that famous American landmark. With a little investigation, however, I found out that it was all just another urban legend. Because the building was built with such an aerodynamic shape, pennies tossed from the observation deck seldom reach the ground. They're caught in updrafts around the building, and end up on one of the building's ledges — usually the eighty-sixth floor, where maintenance workers pick them up as kind of a tip from visitors to the city. You'll certainly never see one embedded in the concrete below, since even if one did make it all the way down, the flat sides of the coin would cause considerable drag as it tumbled. If hit by a one-cent projectile, you might get a sting or a small knot on your noggin, but that would be the extent of the damage.

That's just one of the many interesting tales to be found in New York City. When it comes to ghosts and haunted places, though, there are plenty of those to go around as well. Out of all the places with a ghost story, my favorite was one that was well off the beaten path. So much so that it's very hard to find — on purpose.

This tale concerns a place that served as a speakeasy during Prohibition — a bar named Chumley's. It was purposely hard to find, so that the police wouldn't be able to readily raid it and arrest the revelers inside. In today's world, much like in the past, you must know the famous address of 86 Bedford Street. It is unmarked, which adds to its mystique — no corporate brands or logos here! There are also no windows, and it is soundproof to the street, so going there makes you feel a little like you are sneaking into a forbidden place.

When you walk through the door, you'll find that it's just as interesting on the inside. After going up a few steps and through a curtain, your feet will be kicking up the sawdust on the floor, and you'll immediately notice that the tables aren't the pristine-perfect, cookie-cutter items that you see in many big-city taverns. On the walls are photos and the written works of some of Chumley's most famous clientele: John Steinbeck, Upton Sinclair, F. Scott Fitzgerald, and Orson Wells. The late Mr. Wells is said to have departed New York while leaving a fifteen hundred dollar bar tab. Since a beer was under a buck at the time, he must have bought more than a round or two for the house. One thing missing from the establishment is windows — given that the whole purpose of the place was to hide from the outside world, this makes perfect sense.

Another claim to fame for Chumley's is the origin of the phrase "eighty-six," which was coined during the Prohibition era. If the local police were coming to raid the establishment, the call of "eighty-six" went out in the bar. There was a secret door that opened to 86 Bedford Street, and the patrons would pour out of that exit a few steps ahead of the law. Today, "eighty-sixing" something, at least in the restaurant business, means to get rid of or do away with.

There are several trapdoors in the floor of the restaurant to this day. In the past they were used for hiding liquor, but today they're simply a place of storage for Chumley's. The secrets of the place could fill a book, though. A dumbwaiter in the women's restroom enabled them to escape to safety, and other hidden passageways would take folks from the bar to a cellar beneath a building on nearby Grove Street. It was the perfect place to enjoy an illegal frosty beverage during Prohibition.

Today, you'll still be able to order a cold one at Chumley's, but when it gets crowded — and it tends to do so at times — you'll have to maneuver your way through a maze of people to get to the bar.

And of course, one of the things that caught my eye about Chumley's — other than the beverage selection and the delicious Blue Cheese Burger — were its ghost stories.

The first thing that caught my eye was an article in the New York City University student newspaper. It quoted a bartender in another pub as saying that his place didn't have any ghosts. "I've never seen any here. I used to work at Chumley's — now that place is haunted."

Actually, I was told that every single employee there has at least one ghost story to share. And who knows — these stories may very well be true. Some consider the hauntings there to be a result of the many people who frequented the place for a sip of illegal alcohol during Prohibition. They slipped away from their homes to spend some exciting time during their life, and they may be returning to do so long after their death.

The staff often finds that place settings and even tables have been moved around when the bar wasn't open. These occurrences are blamed on Henrietta Chumley, the wife of the original owner.

No one has actually seen her, but the fact that items move around in the pub can't be ignored. Some of the employees say that she isn't fond of the jukebox either, but so far they've managed to keep it.

Chumley's is so crowded that I doubt the average visitor will have a supernatural experience there. It's already such a sensory overload that the spirits of the place won't have a chance. If you can manage to visit before the crowds arrive, however, you may find that the one-time speakeasy still retains some of the ghosts of its past. In any case, it is well worth a visit, just for the experience. As you're sipping a pint of ale, you may find yourself listening carefully for the sound of the police at the door, ready to pounce on anyone who wasn't near one of the bar's many secret exits. I guarantee it will be one of the best frosty beverages that you ever drink.

Chumley's
86 Bedford St.
(between Barrow and Grove Streets)
New York, NY 10014
(212) 675-4449

The Lights on Brown Mountain

• • • • •

Morganton, North Carolina

 WHILE I WAS writing this book, I ran across one particular phenomenon in many different areas of the country — something colloquially known as "spook lights." Also called "ghost lights," "devil lights," and a dozen other colorful terms, these lights are sometimes blamed on natural elements such as swamp gas, but are occasionally attributed to UFOs or other alien causes. To be honest, about the only thing that I didn't see them accredited to was Bigfoot.

I found the phenomena in Gurden, Arkansas; in Silver Cliff, Colorado; up in Paulding, Michigan; down in Marfa, Texas; even in the Ozark mountains in Joplin, Missouri. Through the years, the occurrence of such lights has been chronicled, studied, photographed, and contemplated — and many go back to the times when only the American Indians inhabited the land. The one thing that most of the lights seemed to have in common was a ghost story, so I thought that I'd pick one of the most interesting places to put in the book. There were many to choose from, but I decided to write about the Brown Mountain Lights, because they occur in a mountain range that is mysterious enough in its own right: the Blue Ridge Mountains.

Many strange things can be found in this range covering several states across the southeast United States, which makes it one of our favorite places to visit. Toward its southern end, a lonesome peak named Fort Mountain contains many secrets. A wall that is comprised of non-native rocks runs eight hundred fifty-five feet along its top. Although there is some controversy as to its origin, most agree that it was probably constructed around the year 500 A.D. for some religious purpose. Local Indian legend tells that it was built for a race of "moon-eyed" people. The wall is constructed so that the sun shines on one side at sunrise and the other at sunset.

You'll also find Blowing Rock in the Blue Ridge Mountains, where a constant wind rushes up from the valley below. Indian legend tells a Romeo/Juliet story of a brave from the plains who fell in love with a girl from the mountains. He climbed up to court her, but when he found that their love was forbidden, he leapt from the rocks. The girl pled with the Great Spirit to save her love, and miraculously he was lifted back up by the wind and placed into her arms. As the story goes, that wind still blows to this day, to the point that when it snows the flakes are swept up — it actually snows upside down!

In the foothills of the Blue Ridge Mountains is Fairy Stone State Park, where the miraculous fairy stones can be found. These rocks bearing a relief of a cross can be found in very few places on Earth, and never in the quantity as in this state park. The stones have criss-crossed staurolite crystals, making a natural cross. They are geological beauties on their own, but there is a local story regarding their origin. In the time before recorded history, it is said that this particular area was inhabited by a race of fairies. They coexisted with men, and knew about the affairs of men. Being creatures of God, the fairies knew when His son came to Earth, and word also reached them about his crucifixion. When they heard the terrible news, it is said that the fairies wept, and where their tears hit the stones of the earth a tiny cross was left.

The Blue Ridge Mountains are filled with many such interesting stories. I mentioned earlier that one of my favorites is the Brown Mountain Lights. You'll find Brown Mountain in Burke County, on the North Carolina end of the Blue Ridge chain.

On our visit to the Blue Ridge Mountains, we knew that we were in for a treat when a black bear scurried across the road in front of us as we drove the winding roads through a light, early morning fog. Since we don't get to see bears where we live, it was wonderful to watch the creature lumbering just at the edge of the fog, as if he were some mythical being that was coming out of an enchanted forest just for us. In only the first hour or so into the trip, we already had stories to tell the folks back home. We planned on spending the day in the mountains, though, so we were hoping for even more wonders.

And we weren't disappointed. We saw all kinds of wildlife, some breathtaking views of the valleys below and the mountains around us, and many sights that would fill this entire book. One thing that was worrying us though was that rain clouds were following us throughout the day. Ever your vigilant journalist, however, we stopped to get some rain gear and pressed on.

Now, there are many places to view the Brown Mountain Lights, but one popular stop is on Highway 181. Go north on it out of Morganton, watching the mileage posts beside the road. At mileage post twenty, there is a large pull-off on the right that offers a very good perspective for viewing the lights.

But what are these celebrated lights? Well, on a clear evening, one can see mysterious, glowing orbs that float down from around Brown Mountain, bobbing up and down. Sometimes they appear in different hues, and their movement is erratic, whizzing around at one moment, almost hovering at another.

There are ghosts legends associated with these lights. The first story comes from the 1850s, when a woman from the area mysteriously disappeared. Although her husband was apparently distraught over the loss, many people thought that he might be responsible. As the Brown Mountain folks continued to search for her, he proclaimed his innocence, until one day he suddenly disappeared, leaving everything at their homestead, as if he'd simply run away. The search tapered off, but as it did, balls of light began to appear in the sky around the searchers. Finally, a group of hunters found the skeleton of a woman who locals assumed to be the missing woman. From that point on, and for the many decades since, the lights have continued to appear.

Yet another story comes from the pre-Civil War area of North Carolina, when a local planter had gone out hunting but failed to return home. A slave was given the order to take a lantern out to the mountain to find the planter and not to return without him. The slave went out searching but never found his charge. Since he couldn't return home without the planter, he continued to look until the exhaustion and the elements finally took his life. His light can supposedly be seen today.

Both are interesting stories, but neither ring with any accuracy. The stories of the Brown Mountain Lights predate the Civil War, and even the settlement of the area. American Indians have stories about the lights on the mountain, and Civil War soldiers reported seeing them as well. There are many contemporary sightings that are well documented, and in fact, the United States government has held three formal investigations.

Some speculation exists. A study was conducted in 1913 where it was concluded that the Brown Mountain Lights were nothing more than locomotive headlights from the Catawba Valley to the south. Three years later, however, a flood swept through the valley and destroyed the railroad bridges. During the time that the railway was being rebuilt, the lights continued to appear.

Others have hypothesized that the lights are the refracted beams of headlights on roads around the mountain, but that theory doesn't hold water either. Long before automobiles rolled off the assembly lines of Michigan, the Catawba and Cherokee Indians regularly saw the lights and believed them to be the spirits of tribal warriors that had been slain in battle.

While scientists try to explain these lights, one thing is certain — they exist. There is no denying that. My only input on the subject is that on a rainy evening in the Blue Ridge Mountains, it's hard to catch a glimpse of these famous lights. I can only say two things. First of all, while you're standing in the darkness beside the road with only the occasional hoot of a great horned owl to break the silence and raindrops are pattering down on your hat, there's only one rational thought: "I wonder where that black bear is that we saw this morning?"

After that, every single thought is, "And what's that noise?"

Brown Mountain
Morganton, North Carolina

A Monster of a Ghost

Liberty Memorial Building — Bismarck, North Dakota

WHEN VISITING North Dakota's Capitol at Bismarck, you'll find a particularly stately building standing on the grounds: the Liberty Memorial Building. The state legislature voted in 1919 to appropriate the funds to build a memorial to the soldiers who gave their lives in the service of our country during what was know at the time as "The Great War." That was what they called World War I, but I guess they didn't realize another one would be rolling around before long.

The memorial was to be a functional building and would be constructed on the grounds of the Capitol. The legislature dictated that its architecture have classic, federal lines to complement the Capitol building, with huge columns and a massive flight of steps leading up to the front doors. They originally budgeted twenty thousand dollars for the project, and work began. The foundation of the building was laid with granite, and the walls on the ground level were made with Bedford Stone from the quarries of Indiana. The inner walls of the first floor lobby were finished with Kasota stone from Minnesota. The floors and stairway feature Italian travertine and Kasota marble, and the list of opulent construction materials goes on and on. As with most government projects, the finishing price tag was higher than originally estimated — more than twice in fact: four hundred fifty thousand dollars.

Once it was complete, the building was a showplace, and it was given the fitting name "Liberty Memorial Building." It became the offices of the North Dakota State Library, the State Supreme Court, and the State Historical Society.

The Historical Society took up several floors, including the basement, and featured a collection of artifacts from all over North Dakota, especially items relating to the pioneers and Indians. An impressive collection of books was also assembled that would rival any library. Some people feel that certain spirits attached to those items may have journeyed to the Liberty Memorial Building with them, because sometime in the 1960s strange happenings began to be noticed by the people there.

Workers and visitors alike would report footsteps and voices in empty hallways, a feeling as if they were being watched as they went about their business, and shadows that seemed to glide through the hallways without being attached to a human.

So many occurrences were reported in the building that the ghost was given a name: The Stack Monster. It was a joking name that allowed the people there to laugh off some of the very real manifestations that continued to occur in the Liberty Memorial Building.

Voices and sounds were some of the most interesting manifestations. An employee working late thought that he was alone on his floor, when he heard the distinct cough of a person not far away. Thinking it odd that someone else would be there, he went to investigate, only to find that he was the only living soul in the place.

Certainly he could have imagined the cough, but there were other stories of voices in the building. Two employees of the

Historical Society were working alone one night, and one had ventured downstairs to the basement. Through the silence of the halls there, he heard a man call his name, and then say, "Come here!" Assuming that it was his friend, he went to see what he wanted, but discovered that the other fellow was up on the second floor and couldn't possibly have called him.

Working late in the building seemed to be a good way to encounter the spirit — or at least receive a warning from him. More than one person has been toiling away after hours only to have the sudden, distinct thought "Get out of the building NOW!" It was such a disturbing event that more often than not, the person would grab his briefcase and leave immediately.

The Stack Monster, as everyone in the building continued to call the spirit, was certainly no monster in the classic sense of the word. In fact, the ghost was glimpsed a few times walking the halls and seemed to be the spirit of a man. On other occasions when he wasn't actually seen, his footsteps were heard echoing through empty hallways.

One can only speculate whether this was actually a phantom attached to the collection of historical memorabilia or the ghost of an employee who had died but wanted to continue working there. No matter what the explanation, the Stack Monster was experienced by enough people to confirm that something strange was going on at the Liberty Memorial Building.

In 1981, the State Historical Society was moved to the new North Dakota Heritage Center, including all of the artifacts, displays, and books. The Liberty Memorial Building became the home of the North Dakota Department of Tourism. The reports of the Stack Monster have quieted, and he doesn't seem to have made the move to the new building either. Whatever occurred during the process of changing locations must have quieted the spirit, although the basement of the Liberty Memorial is still a little creepy, and there are those who won't go there alone — in fear, perhaps, of stirring the Stack Monster once again.

Liberty Memorial Building
604 East Boulevard Ave.
Bismarck, ND 58595
(701) 224-2525

Major Buxton… The Man, The Cat

─── ◦ ◦ ● ◦ ◦ ───

The Buxton Inn — Granville, Ohio

WHEN I'M OUT on the road, one of the most exciting things for me to find is an old, historic inn where I can spend a night or two. Sure, modern hotels are sometimes more plush, but there's nothing like standing on a century-old floor, gazing out of a window across the lush, green countryside, and wondering whose footprints you might be standing in. Patriots, presidents, even paupers from years past might have taken in that same view — and so will people for the next hundred years. I found many jewels in the course of this book, but let me add another one to that list: the Buxton Inn, located in the quaint little village of Granville, Ohio.

Before even entering the building, you'll notice how lovely the grounds are — with bubbling fountains and colorful, fragrant flowers. It's located in the heart of historic downtown Granville, which makes it a perfect home base for exploring the city.

What I found most intriguing, however, was the history of the Buxton Inn. It is almost two hundred years old, making it

Granville's oldest business and Ohio's oldest continuously operated inn. The old place certainly has some stories to tell.

The structure was originally built in 1812 to be used as a stagecoach stop. When travelers on the stage line wanted to stop for the evening, innkeeper Orrin Granger could provide them a bed for the night and a mug of ale to take the edge off the day. The Tavern, as it was known back then, was also a place for the local military to meet, since Orrin Granger was an officer during the War of 1812.

In 1858 The Tavern changed hands, and it was known as the Dilley House for a while. The inn's namesake, Major Horton Buxton, would come to acquire it in 1865 and reportedly had the inn longer than any other owner. The innkeeper during the 1920s was Mary Stevens Sweet, and in 1934, Ethyl "Bonnie Bounell" Houston purchased the business and kept it until her death in 1961. It passed to a Miss Nell Schoeller next, who kept it until 1972 when the current owners, Orville and Audrey Orr, approached her with an offer to buy the Buxton Inn. The Orrs have done a masterful job of restoring the inn and preserving its history.

And what a history it has! Visitors include the ninth president of the United States, William Henry Harrison, who stayed there during the War of 1812 when he was a general in the army. He probably did so because the original owner, Orrin Granger, was an officer as well. Buxton Inn lore says that General Harrison rode his horse up the stairs to a ballroom on the second floor.

Other presidents who visited the inn were Abraham Lincoln and William McKinley. If you believe in coincidences, all three happened to have died in office — certainly nothing to do with the Buxton Inn, of course. Distinguished guests weren't limited to the presidency. Henry Ford stayed at the inn every time he came to visit his niece who was attending Denison University. It is said that Ford loved the place so much that he wanted to purchase it, carefully take it apart, and reconstruct it at Greenfield Village, a historic community that he was building.

John Phillips Sousa, writer of "Stars and Stripes Forever" — which was the melody for the school song of my high school alma mater — stayed at the Buxton Inn, as did Harriet Beecher Stowe, the civil rights activist and writer of *Uncle Tom's Cabin*.

The inn has more than a guest book full of prestigious names, however. It also has the reputation for housing a ghost or two. The first documentation of a haunting at the Buxton Inn came from 1932, when the alumni newsletter from nearby Denison University featured an article titled, "The House the Ghost Built." It documented some of the early twentieth century hauntings, as experienced by Mary Stevens Sweet.

You don't have to look back that far for ghost stories from the inn, however. They are plentiful and have been well documented. When the current owners purchased the property, haunted encounters began to happen almost immediately. A common occurrence was the opening and closing of doors in an area where no one was present. Footsteps were — and still are — heard in empty hallways, an earmark of many haunted old buildings. Many of these experiences have been attributed to the original owner, Orrin Granger, throughout the years.

It may be that some of the other former owners are showing up for a visit as well, though. Ms. Houston owned a tabby cat that she named Major Buxton, and together they've been spotted wandering the halls of the inn, especially on the second floor. Major Buxton — the cat, not the owner — has even been seen on his own, sitting out on the steps just as he probably did when he was alive. Ms. Houston confines her activities, for the most part, to the second floor.

Another apparition is attributed to Major Buxton himself — the owner, not the cat. He seems to have laid claim to the first floor, where he can be heard still pacing through the rooms of his inn. It has had several different owners since his time, so he may simply be returning to make sure that the high standards he set are still being followed.

At the Buxton Inn today, that's not a problem. The major would be proud.

The Buxton Inn
313 East Broadway
Granville, OH 43023
(740) 587-0001
www.buxtoninn.com

The Playful Spirit of Little Augusta

·◦●◦·

The Stone Lion Inn — Guthrie, Oklahoma

I TRAVEL TO Oklahoma at least once a year. Not only is it a beautiful state, but it is also the home of a writer's conference in Oklahoma City that I consider to be one of the best in the country. As a writer myself, that appeals to me, but an extra added bonus is having the opportunity to drive across the state and simply soak in its beauty.

As a child, my family spent many weekends camping at Beaver's Bend near Broken Bow, Oklahoma. During those years, I think that my friend Mike and I explored every trail in that part of the state. From memories of my adolescence to the last trip there a short while ago, I have a special fondness for the state.

If you happen to travel half an hour north of Oklahoma City, you'll find the city of Guthrie — the Capital of Oklahoma. Okay, not today, maybe, but at least once upon a time.

On April 22, 1889, the government began a push to dispose of the unassigned land in Oklahoma, so when the sun came up that morning, a horde of fifty thousand people had crowded along a specified line, waiting for the signal. At high noon, the blue-clad military fired cannons and rifles and sounded trumpets to signal the start of the land run. As each person reached an available one hundred sixty-acre plot of land, he would drive a stake in the ground bearing his name. Many left family members to guard their claim while they hurried to the land office to register their claim, and the "Eighty-Niners" became a part of the state's history. If you'd like to see a portrayal of this event, check out the Tom Cruise movie *Far and Away*. That event was factual, and it happened right around Guthrie.

In 1907 when the Oklahoma territory became a state, Guthrie was chosen as the state capital. The honor was short-lived, however, because on June 11, 1910, it was officially moved to Oklahoma City. It was an unfortunate event for the city of Guthrie, because the power shift severely hurt the economy. Many beautiful homes and buildings were constructed during the capital period, many of which have been preserved and restored. In fact, the historic district of Guthrie is one of the largest in the nation.

One of the historic buildings in Guthrie is now the Stone Lion Inn, built in 1907 during the land rush days — although it wasn't always a welcoming bed and breakfast. It was originally a majestic mansion that served the Fred E. Houghton family. Mr. and Mrs. Houghton were blessed with several children and led a wonderful life there, until tragedy befell the family. Their eight-year-old daughter Augusta contracted pertussis, commonly known as whooping cough. Although in today's world children are immunized and the disease is preventable, prior to the vaccine's discovery in 1940, more than ten thousand people died from the disease. The family was understandably concerned for her life.

Even though there was no preventative, there were medicines to treat the disease. A dose of such a medication was given to the girl, but a terrible mistake occurred. It was the wrong type of medicine, and little Augusta died.

The Houghton family pulled together and overcame the tragedy, and continued to live in their beautiful home. Eventually, the house changed hands, and was even used as a funeral home for a period of time. In 1986, however, it was lovingly converted into the luxurious bed and breakfast that it is today. As you drive up to the inn, you'll notice the ample porch that is the perfect place to curl up with a book and a cup of coffee.

The reputation of the inn is not only national, but has spread around the world — it has been featured in publications such as *Good Housekeeping*, the *Wall Street Journal*, and even the *London Daily Telegraph*. It has been given accolades such as *Oklahoma Gazette*'s "Best of Oklahoma," and has been featured on CNN and CBS.

One of the specialties of the inn is murder mysteries, and as a guest you may be a victim, a suspect, or even the murderer! Whether you visit the Stone Lion Inn for a carefree weekend or a fun-filled whodunit, you will quickly fall in love with the place.

While you're being pampered there, however, you might want to keep a watch out for a supernatural visitor or two. Since the bed and breakfast was first opened, there have been subtle indications that residents from the home's past are occasionally dropping in for a visit.

Phantom footsteps have been heard, accompanied by the sound of a door opening and closing. In the beginning it so alarmed the current owners that they summoned the police, who found nothing to explain the sounds.

The mysterious noises continued, with one of the most active places being the back stairway. After ten o'clock in the evening, someone can occasionally be heard climbing the steps.

Another strange event happened in the third floor bedroom of the current owner's youngest son. Before going to bed, all of his toys had been neatly placed into the closet and the doors closed. When he woke up the next morning, the toys were scattered all around the room as if an unseen child had spent all night playing with them. Many people think that little Augusta is returning to the house where she passed away — if so, she was probably delighted with the playthings brought in by the new owners. She may occasionally bring her own toys with her on her visits, though, since the sound of a wooden ball rolling down the hardwood hallway floors can sometimes be heard.

Augusta may still be wandering the different rooms of the Stone Lion Inn, because guests have reported the intense feeling that a child is in their room, even though it is empty. Others say that they have awakened in the night to the sensation of having the covers tucked around them or felt the romping of a child playing on the bed where they were sleeping.

Little Augusta isn't the only spirit at the inn. Her father, Fred E. Houghton, also makes his presence known there. One of the ways that he does this is by the smell of his pipe tobacco, usually in the front sitting rooms — it is immediately noticeable since the Stone Lion is a non-smoking facility. His figure has even been seen down in the basement. Whether he's there to check on Augusta or simply visiting the old home on his own, visitors might just run across the spirit of Mr. Houghton.

Or you may not encounter any spirits there at all during your visit — the only thing that you'll be guaranteed of is a good time!

Stone Lion Inn
1016 West Warner
Guthrie, OK 73044
(405) 282-0012
www.stonelioninn.com

Shanghaied!

—◦ ● ● ● ◦—

The Shanghai Tunnels — Portland, Oregon

AH, TIME FOR a weary traveler like yourself to wet your whistle with a cold drink at a local tavern. Finding yourself in the Chinatown area of Portland, you step through the door of the Snug Harbor Saloon, stride confidently to the bar, and order yourself a frosty beverage. The barkeep smiles as he delivers a drink with a foaming head and makes idle conversation as you gulp it down.

Odd. It has a strange, bitter taste to it. As you start to question the bartender about this, your vision blurs and the room begins to slowly swirl around you. With a painful thump, your body hits the floor and a man nudges your arms and legs up next to your torso with the toe of his foot. He nods at the bartender, who thumps on the floor with a wooden stick. There are sudden noises below the floor, and in an instant, you are plummeting into a world of blackness and pain. Your life will never be the same — you've been shanghaied!

Portland, Oregon, was a bustling river port over one hundred fifty years ago. Ships would dock there every day before sailing the Willamette River and "crossing the bar" into the Pacific

Ocean. In the 1850s, there weren't enough sailors to man all the ships heading out for trade with the Orient. The ship captains needed a full complement of men before sailing on, so they turned to the terrible practice of dealing with dastardly men who provided the able bodies that they needed for a price — about fifty dollars each.

The practice was called "shanghaiing" after the city of Shanghai, China, because most of the ships were headed to the Far East. The average encounter played out in the following manner. A man would walk into one of the seedier establishments of the city: a bar, a brothel, a gambling hall, or someplace worse. After he ordered a drink, it was served with a little something extra; some type of knock-out additive was included, usually an opium-based derivative. The other patrons would just think that he was simply drunk as slipped off of his stool and onto the floor. Once he was in place, someone from the establishment would signal the "crimp" below, who would throw the lever to open the "deadfall," which was a trapdoor to quickly and quietly bring the victim underground.

The crimp, who was for all intents and purposes a kidnapper, would have positioned a mattress below the deadfall so as not to damage the merchandise. With the victim below ground, the door would be closed and no one in the establishment would be the wiser. If the ship was ready to set sail, he would be carried directly there. If not, he would be put in a holding cell in the underground passages. Drugs would be administered through his food and water to keep him docile until it was time to sell the poor fellow to a sea captain. Because many tried to escape, the kidnappers would immediately take their shoes away. The floors of the passages were sprinkled with broken glass, making a getaway a painful and bloody process.

Finally, the shanghaied man was delivered to the ship that would become his home for the next several years. He was knocked out for this part of the journey so that there would be no arguments — in fact, often the victim would not wake up until the ship was at least a day's journey out on the ocean. From that point, there was a very basic choice to make: work or die. The vast majority of these men would never be heard from again, simply disappearing from their previous life after a simple drink at an ordinary Portland tavern.

To facilitate this terrible practice, a network of tunnels was developed under the city. They weren't only used to grab unfortunate men, however. Women were captured in a very similar manner and were sold into a terrible life of slavery. Portland, Oregon, was an epicenter for the organized kidnapping and selling of both men and women from the 1850s through the 1940s, earning it the title the "Unheavenly City" or the "Forbidden City." Sailors called it the "most dangerous port in the world," because if they were on shore leave they might very well wake up on a different ship bound for the Orient.

Today, you can walk though this network of tunnels and see them for yourself. You can witness the cages where men were kept before being shipped off to their fate. There are stacks of shoes that were seized from the victims so that they couldn't run away over the hallways strewn with glass. Under some of Portland's current businesses, there are still trapdoors where the victims were captured.

Traversing the tunnels would be very dangerous today, but fortunately there are experts that can safely and efficiently lead visitors on a tour through Portland's Shanghai Tunnels. Your guides can give extensive details of the history of the catacombs, along with a ghost story or two. You see, with all of the human suffering that took place there, these underground tunnels still retain a few visitors from the past. Many people who were taken there never came out. Although the crimps positioned mattresses under the deadfalls, occasionally an injury would occur, and a wounded victim was of no use — a sea captain would only pay for healthy, able-bodied men. When that happened, the man was simply killed and the body dumped.

There were other tragedies that occurred underground. While a group of men were partying the night away at the Snug Harbor Saloon, one happened to walk past an open doorway and saw that in the chamber below, there were several unguarded barrels, presumably containing whiskey for the saloon. He called to his companions, and they ran down the stairs to enjoy the free beverage. Several hours later, the notorious crimp Joseph "Bunco" Kelly was making his way through the catacombs and came upon the revelers — all lying dead on the tunnel floor. He discovered that they had been drinking the contents of the barrels — not whiskey but rather embalming fluid from the funeral home next door. As the legend goes, Kelly called his crimp friends and together they carried the men to the riverfront, selling them to a captain in need of hands. He gave his assurance that the men would be easy to deal with, since they were "dead drunk."

But what spirits have been encountered in the Shanghai Tunnels? Actually, there seems to be quite a bit of activity. Visitors sometimes report the feeling of an unseen person brushing against them, as if a ghostly passerby touched them.

Along with the musty smells of the catacombs, people have also said that they have walked into pockets of tobacco smoke, as if they were in the presence of a very heavy smoker — although you aren't allowed to smoke on the tours. It is as if one of the crimps from the bygone days is passing through, in search of a mark to carry to the riverfront.

And the voices… many visitors have reported the sound of human voices echoing through the cavernous passageways. You have to be careful when reporting this, because depending on where you are, it is possible that you have wandered underneath a crowded business on the street level above. Still, the sounds that some report are from within the tunnels themselves — people speaking frankly, with others crying out in agony in a pleading tone.

When you visit Portland, you may or may not encounter the spirits of the Shanghai Tunnels. They are definitely worth a visit, however, if only for the history alone. Nowhere else in America was this terrible practice exercised with such a fierce intensity. Literally thousands of people disappeared from their everyday lives, and it may be that a few still return to the place where their destiny changed forever.

Nowadays, it is perfectly safe to enjoy a beverage in one of Portland's Old Town establishments. While the trapdoors — the deadfalls — may still be in the floor, they are hardly ever used anymore!

If you tour the Shanghai Tunnels, one more thing that you'll see is the wooden statue of a cigar store Indian. As the legend goes, one crimp who was even more unscrupulous than most was selling victims to a sea captain who was desperate to increase his head count for the upcoming voyage. He didn't have any more unfortunate humans to peddle, so he took a wooden cigar store Indian and wrapped it in a blanket, then carried it onto the ship. He collected the money from the captain, but warned him that this particular fellow had been heavily sedated and should be allowed to sleep it off for a couple of days. The ship set sail, and by the time that the captain discovered that he himself had been a victim of the crimp, it was too late to turn around. With a hefty curse, he threw the wooden warrior overboard and continued on toward the Orient. The Indian washed up at Astoria, Oregon, and was eventually returned to his home in Portland. You can visit him where he now stands guard — in the Portland Underground: the Shanghai Tunnels.

The Shanghai Tunnels
c/o The Cascade Geographic Society
Portland, Oregon
(503) 622-4798

The Spirits of Devil's Den

Gettysburg, Pennsylvania

OVER THE YEARS, I've seen any number of "top ten most haunted places" lists on television shows and in printed articles. These are always determined by the person doing the writing, of course, but there seems to be one location that makes it every single time: the Gettysburg Battlefield.

And why wouldn't the place be haunted? After all, it is considered to be the worst battle ever fought by American forces — an assessment that I'm inclined to agree with. In three days' time, well over fifty thousand soldiers were killed, wounded, or captured. The pain and suffering on that battlefield was immeasurable — and the horrors during the conflict shook even the most seasoned of veterans.

Entire books have been dedicated to the ghosts of that battlefield, so while I was researching this chapter I had to wonder why I'd even attempt to capture a small segment of the legends here. While walking the sacred, grassy hills of one of the battlegrounds, I felt the somber silence like a blanket, and knew that each rock, stone, and tree must have its own story to tell.

As you stroll through the fields of Gettysburg, you will find places with familiar names from the history books: Round Top, Little Round Top, Cemetery Ridge, the Peach Orchard, the Wheat Field, and one with the ominous name Devil's Den. The latter intrigued me greatly — it is a group of huge boulders cropping out from the ground at odd angles. From one view, it looks like a rock fortress; from another, some sort of mystic place, as if Stonehenge had somehow collapsed. The thing that intrigues me about Devil's Den is the jumble of historical facts around the fighting there. Two or three very respected historians may give two or three different accounts of Devil's Den on July 2, 1863, and exactly what happened on that bloody day.

One account seems to have at least some degree of accuracy. On July 2, 1863, Devil's Den was held by the Union forces, including Brigadier General Hobart Ward's Brigade and Captain James Smith's 4th New York Battery.

That afternoon, under a hail of bullets and artillery, several Confederate forces stormed the natural fortress. These included Benning's brigade of Georgia, the 4th Texas Regiment of General Jerome Robertson's brigade, and the 44th Alabama Regiment of General Evander Law's brigade.

The fighting was fierce — Union riflemen hid among the rocks of Devil's Den and picked off the attackers in what would come to be known as "the slaughtering pit." The 4th New York Battery did its own damage with heavier weaponry. The steady stream of rebel soldiers eventually captured several of the large guns, however, but not without heavy losses. The Confederate soldiers eventually made their way into the belly of Devil's Den, sending the Union troops scampering out over the rocks in all directions. Those who were cornered in the nooks and crannies were quickly taken prisoner, and CSA snipers took their positions to support the other battles going on around them, specifically picking off Union troops on Little Round Top. Their rifles were quite deadly, so a concentrated effort by shooters from Little Round Top to oust the rebels was launched. By the end of the day, Devil's Den was once again in Federal hands, and the battlefield of Gettysburg was silent, waiting for the sunrise, and the final day of battle.

Tours of the battlefield began very soon after the Civil War, and from some of those original accounts we get a very good picture of what happened on July 2. This brief passage quoted from *The Occasional Writings of Isaac Moorhead, With a Sketch of His Life* (ed., A. H. Caughey, Erie, 1882) is a description written by Mr. Moorhead as he toured Gettysburg with a guide named Mr. Frey:

"As we approached Round Top it was at once evident that it was the key of the whole position — that point lost and all was lost. Driving our carriage down the rocky lane that leads from the turnpike to Round Top, we soon reached the base. Dismounting among the rocks, we saw some bones of a rebel, with shreds of his 'butternut' clothing. We passed through the woods filled with rocks, and ascended the Round Top. The summit is clear of trees, but they are scattered on the sides. On a large rock near the summit is chiseled the inscription; 'Col. Strong Vincent fell here com'g 3rd, Brig. lst div. 5th corps, July 2d, 1863.' Standing on the rock and looking down into the valley, Mr. Frey called my attention to the 'Devil's Den,' which consisted of two immense rocks standing up side by side, with a small but convenient opening between them. Across the top was another immense rock. The opening was in such a position that neither shot nor shell, although freely thrown at the rebel sharp-shooter occupying this place, could reach him. The story goes (and I deem it an exceedingly plausible one, and Mr. Frey says he does not doubt it), that Col. Vincent was hit by this sharp-shooter in the 'Devil's Den.' After repeated efforts to dislodge him, two of Berdan's sharpshooters were called up and the locality of the fellow pointed out to them. One of them slipped down to the friendly cover of a large Whitewood tree, to the right of the Vincent rock, and flanking the opening of the 'Devil's Den.' Here waiting until the rebel reloaded his gun, and coming cautiously to the end of the rock, he took deliberate aim and sent the rebel to his long home. This [Berdan] sharp-shooter has been at Gettysburg since the battle, and went with Mr. Frey to all these localities. The rebels grave is just at the mouth of the den, and his boots I saw lying just within the den. Passing down to the vast rocks, scattered about in the valley at the foot of the mountain, which afforded such excellent lurking spots for the enemy's sharp-shooters, we were told by our guide that many wounded rebels had crawled under these rocks for safety. After the battle heavy rains set in and drowned many of them, and the current of water brought them to view. Others there were undiscovered until the flesh had fallen from their bones. Here, in a secluded spot among the rocks, I found the bones of a rebel just as he had fallen. Picking up one of his shoes to remove the string, to tie together some little trees, the bones of his foot tumbled out. It was a 'Georgia state shoe' made from canvas, with leather tips and heel stiffeners. From among his ribs I picked up a battered minie ball which doubtless caused his death. Moving aside a flat stone, Mr. Frey showed us the grinning face and skull of a rebel. Some of them in this rocky part of the field have very shallow graves."

It wasn't long until such visitors began to notice strange happenings around the massive rocks of Devil's Den. In fact, a story spread by some of the tour guides lent an air of mystery to the place from the day of the battle. As the story was told, when the Union Army recaptured the Den, they found that up to fifty or so Confederate sharpshooters were laying there dead — but not a single bullet hole could be found in any of their bodies. It was as if some supernatural force, if not the devil himself, had taken the lives of the rebel soldiers. Historians who were looking for plausible explanations for such a discovery determined that the loud explosions on the rock walls around them gave the soldiers killing concussions, leaving them dead without being shot. As it turns out, however, neither of these is true. The Confederate solders were picked off by gunshot, as described by Mr. Moorhead's writing above.

Still, the mysterious arrangements of the rocks easily led to such stories. One fact about the place, however, is that many people who visit the location have camera problems. The shutter won't work, batteries die out suddenly, and some equipment has even come apart in the owner's hands. Many people believe that this is caused by a soldier whose body was mishandled by photographers right after the battle. Two photographers, in fact: Alexander Gardner and Timothy O'Sullivan. As the story goes, the men were chronicling the aftermath of the battle and snapped a photo of a dead Confederate soldier lying on the southern slope of Devil's Den. After walking around a bit more, they thought that a better photo would be much better inside of the rock formation at a place nicknamed "Sharpshooter's Den," which was the inner sanctum of the rocks. They dragged the soldier's body inside and arranged it there for the photo, which was subsequently published. Because the sanctity of his death was violated, supposedly the spirit of the soldier interferes with visitors today who are there to take photos. No matter what the reason is, however, one fact remains: People often have problems with their cameras at Devil's Den.

That's not the only strange thing that happens there, however. People walking through the passageways between the rocks often hear someone moving around behind them. When they turn, there is no one there. The phantom soldiers who lost their life seem to still be walking the stone corridors of Devil's Den. Since both Union and Confederate soldiers died together on this particular plot of land, perhaps they are now at peace together.

Devil's Den
Gettysburg Battlefield
Gettysburg, Pennsylvania

The Textile Baron's Ghost

━━━━━━━━━━═•◉●◉•═━━━━━━━━━━

Brookside Manor — Wakefield, Rhode Island

 THERE IS ONE THING that is incredibly impressive about Rhode Island: Although it is a small state, it has a huge history behind it. It is easy to get lost in the tales of the state — after all, it was one of the thirteen original colonies to renounce its allegiance to Great Britain. There are many interesting places to visit while you're knocking around the state, but I have to recommend a visit to the city of Wakefield, and particularly a stop at the historic old Brookside Manor. Once a beautiful home, it is now an inn for travelers in search of a comfortable place to spend the evening.

When it was built back in 1690, long before the revolt of the colonies, it was a well-appointed manor house that was part of an eight-acre estate. It was built by a gentleman named Thomas Mumford, Jr. It was a two-story home constructed around a central chimney, and was described in a 1695 publication of "A Descriptione of the Country of New England," Throughout the early years, it changed hands several times, all to prominent New England families such as the Congdons, the Dockrays, and the Watsons. With each family, the house was modified to accommodate their individual needs.

In 1921, the house was purchased by Charles Fletcher, a giant in the textile industry, and he hired nationally known architect Norman Morrisson Isham, the "Father of the Colonial Revival." Not completely satisfied with the results, Fletcher then hired architect Albert Harkness to increase the size of the house, while maintaining its colonial appearance.

During Fletcher's ownership, the estate is credited with helping to save the city of Wakefield when the great hurricane of 1938 hit. The town's water supply failed, and it was only because of Brookside Manor's well that the people were able to obtain drinking water.

When Charles Fletcher died in 1965, the manor house was sold to the Tarzwell family, who held it for thirty-one years. In 1996 the current owners purchased the house and opened its charms to the public as an inn. With its architecture and history, Brookside Manor is a true American gem, and it has fittingly been nominated for listing on the National Register of Historic Places.

One spirit keeps making his presence known again and again at Brookside, and through the years, most people have come to believe that it is Charles Fletcher who has simply come back to check on the home that he loved so much.

Not only does he play harmless pranks, like taking pillows off the beds, only to later return them to the guests, but he also keeps a close watch on any renovations going on at his manor house.

Charles' presence is especially prominent in the oldest part of the house, the structure that was there before his architects expanded it. In fact, a former innkeeper there was staying in one of the older rooms after the death of her husband. The spirit of Charles Fletcher appeared at her bedside, waking her up, only to ask if she was all right living in the manor house by herself. Although she'd never put much stock in the ghost stories associated with the place, she was an instant believer. She also found a sense of comfort, though, that her husband was doing just fine on the other side. Charles' visit proved to be an incredible comfort for her.

Workers in the house especially report seeing a man pacing by as if checking their work, so Mr. Fletcher must still care a great deal about the inn. And why not — after all, it is a wonderful place to spend a relaxing evening. When you stay at Brookside Manor, you'll have your choice of five distinctive rooms, and the landscaped gardens surrounding the house are perfect for an afternoon stroll — you'll love the bubbling stream and pond on the property.

Just don't go making any modifications to your room while you're there. If you do, then you may very well encounter the spirit of Charles Fletcher, stopping by to see just exactly what you are doing to his beloved inn.

Brookside Manor
380-B Post Road
Wakefield, RI 02879
(401) 788-3527

The Little Girl Ghost

The Rutledge Victorian Guest House —
Charleston, South Carolina

IT'S TIME FOR another trip to the Deep South, this time stopping in the coastal city of Charleston, South Carolina — home of Fort Sumter, where on April 12, 1861, the first shots of the Civil War were fired. Brigadier General Beauregard, who commanded the Confederate troops at Charleston, had his batteries open fire on the fort, and by 2:30 p.m. the next day the Union forces had surrendered. There were no casualties in the brief battle, although it was the opening to what would be America's bloodiest war.

Charleston is also the center for many legendary ghosts — in fact, there are several ghost tours that wind through the streets with tales of haunted houses, jails, and graveyards.

One of the places that you may pass in your wanderings is on Rutledge Avenue. It is a colorful house that is a "painted lady," which is a name for a Victorian style home that is painted in at least three colors that accentuate the ruffles and flourishes of the architecture.

You'll notice how inviting it is as soon as you arrive — the beautifully trimmed home, the shade of the magnolia tree, the sweeping staircase to the front door. One of my absolute favorite features of the place is a one hundred twenty-foot wraparound verandah; it is the perfect place to put your feet up, sip a cool mint julep, and watch the world go by. The owners have placed many inviting chairs, recliners, and rockers there that can easily tempt a weary traveler off of his feet.

Inside the house, not only will you find the rooms decorated in classic Victorian décor, but you'll also find a welcoming atmosphere. There are fresh-baked cookies just waiting to be sampled, books and board games placed around the house, even brandy and chocolates as you turn in at night.

As wonderful as it is now as a bed and breakfast, its history is an interesting part of Charleston's lore.

Originally known as the Brodie-Pinkussohn house, it was built in 1887 and was once the home to a Charleston tobacco baron. This fact is apparent by the elegance of the inn as it appears today.

A terrible tragedy occurred at the house, however, that would leave an impression on the place forever. There was a daughter named Sarah, a typical young girl with all of the accoutrements of a well-to-do family. She had dolls, toys, and even the highest room in the house with a beautiful view of Charleston. One sleepy day in the city, a fire broke out in the Brodie-Pinkussohn house. The residents escaped to the street below, only to make a horrible discovery: Young Sarah was still upstairs, trapped in her bedroom by the raging inferno. The family watched helplessly as the local fire brigade valiantly fought the blaze and finally managed to save the home. Their daughter was not so fortunate, however. Poor Sarah perished that terrible day.

The parents, unable to get over her death, boarded up the top floor of the house — it remained that way for eight long decades.

In the 1980s, the house was purchased and transformed into a beautiful inn; a "painted lady" for the city of Charleston. The top floor was opened once again, and restoration returned Sarah's old room to its original elegance.

As guests began to occupy the top floor, however, a strange thing was noticed — Sarah sometimes returned for a quiet visit to her old room.

Visitors have been nudged and poked, and their bedcovers pulled. It is not a frightening experience, simply a curious little girl returning to her quarters to find out who might be sleeping there.

For some reason, when Sarah comes back to visit her child-hood home, she has a strong aversion to light. She often flips off lights as she passes along, some say because they remind her of the flames that took her young life.

Sarah doesn't limit herself to gentle nudges and the flicking of a light switch, however. The most dramatic manifestation of the little girl is when Sarah appears as she did so many years ago — a beautiful young lady with curls and a gentle smile, looking out of the window of the top floor that oversees the stairway. As guests have climbed the majestic staircase up to their room, some have reported her peeking through the window down at them.

The Rutledge Victorian Guest House is no place to be afraid, for there aren't any frightening spirits there; just a little girl ghost, who occasionally comes back home to the place that she remembers so well.

The Rutledge Victorian Guest House
Charleston Historic District
114 Rutledge Ave.
Charleston, SC 29401
(843) 722-7551
(888) 722-7553
www.charlestonvictorian.com

The Ghost of the Gunman

Bullock Hotel — Deadwood, South Dakota

NOW, I'M NOT much of a gambler. I'll occasionally sit down at a low-stakes blackjack table to try my luck, and every now and then I will do okay. Of course, when I do, I'm so happy that I usually end up tipping the dealer as much as I won. If I'm walking through a casino and pass a slot machine that catches my eye, I may put a few dollars in. By the time I've finished, usually I'm just happy if I've broken even. I'm just not that lucky a person when it comes to gaming.

My wife is the polar opposite — sit her down in front of a video poker machine, and she's a pinball wizard. On our last visit she walked away with two hundred dollars from a single game, and before that, one fast hand paid her eighty bucks. Me? Well, I'm happy if my allotted budget lasts the evening.

Whether you're winning or losing, though, casinos are exciting places. When you're looking to combine a little gaming with a few ghosts, one of the best places to go is north to the legendary city of Deadwood, South Dakota, and visit the Bullock Hotel.

It is named after Deadwood's first sheriff, Seth Bullock, who was born in Ontario, Canada. At the age of sixteen he headed for the United States and settled in Montana. Seth was a natural

193

leader, and was elected to several civic offices while he was in his twenties. He was soon appointed to be the sheriff of the Montana Territory. Seth gained quite a reputation with a gun, but his stern demeanor earned him the legend of being "the sheriff whose gaze could stop a fight."

Stories began to drift in about the huge gold strikes in the Black Hills of the Dakotas, however, and Seth began to look in that direction. He and a friend, Sol Star, moved to Deadwood to open a hardware business to supply the many prospectors there. Legend has it that when they got to town they brought a wagonload of supplies, and they pulled onto the side of the street and started selling. Their store actually opened in 1876.

The law in Deadwood was kept by Wild Bill Hickok, a legendary lawman who had traveled with Buffalo Bill's Wild West Show. He and his contemporaries, "Colorado" Charlie Utter and Martha "Calamity Jane" Canary, were some of the most colorful figures in town. In August of 1876, however, Wild Bill was shot dead by the outlaw Jack McCall, and Seth Bullock was drafted into that position. To keep the peace, he hired several fast-draw, no-nonsense deputies, and his transition into the position was unchallenged.

While he was sheriff, his hardware store was nearly destroyed by fire, so he and his partner had to rebuild. After careful consideration, they made it much bigger and better, and then opened the new structure as the sixty-four-room Bullock Hotel. It was so modern that it had one bathroom on *every single floor,* an amenity that was unheard of at the time. It soon had the reputation as one of the most extravagant hotels in the Badlands. Both Bullock and his hotel prospered for many years.

While the gunman was able to fight off the fiercest of foes, there was one that he could not stand up against: Cancer took his life in September of 1919. He died in Room 211 of the hotel that he loved so much, and he was buried on the mountainside above Deadwood.

It could be, however, that he still makes an occasional visit to the Bullock Hotel to see how things are going. His presence has been felt at various places in the hotel, especially some of the guest rooms, the second and third floor hallways, and Bully's Restaurant — named for Theodore Roosevelt, a close friend of Seth's. One of the most common occurrences is a strange feeling in the air and the sense that someone is there watching as you walk across an empty room. Occasionally, it is more than just an eerie feeling, however; the figure of a man has been glimpsed in one of the forenamed places, simply walking along or stepping quickly out of view. Even if you don't see the tall gentleman, you may very well hear his footsteps walking down the hallway.

The staff reports a strange occurrence that happens occasionally in Room 305. When the chambermaids go into the room to make it up, an old clock that otherwise doesn't work sometimes begins to chime. Since Seth Bullock was known to run a very efficient hotel, it may be that he is sounding the chime to let the staff know that he is watching the clock.

Another room that is reported to be particularly active is number 211, the very room where Seth passed away. Visitors to this room have even captured images on film showing a white fog hovering over the bed.

Given my mediocre luck at the gaming tables, you're more likely to find me over in Bully's or at Seth's Cellar Restaurant having a thick, juicy steak. Seth himself, on the other hand, you may run across at several places in the Bullock Hotel, and when visiting I'm going to be sure to watch my manners and behavior — I don't want to catch one of those legendary stern gazes of the gunfighter.

The Historic Bullock Hotel
633 Main St.
Deadwood, SD 57732
(800) 336-1876
(605) 578-1745
www.heartofdeadwood.com

The Gorilla Pants Ghost

Falcon Manor — McMinnville, Tennessee

SOME PLACES TRY to downplay their hauntings, while others celebrate them. The latter is certainly the case with Falcon Manor, one of Tennessee's treasures. The inn has always played host to weddings and family celebrations, and has an award-winning murder mystery dinner theater titled "Murder at the Manor." The latest Halloween addition to the place that bills itself as "the Victorian mansion where history is fun" is a new interactive show — "Ghosts at the Manor." In the program, the manor staff portrays the "host ghosts," and the guests play various other members of the spirit world.

At Falcon Manor, though, there are some spirits that don't need human actors to play their part; they seem to be doing just fine on their own. One of them is thought to be the original owner of the place, a southern gentleman named Clay Faulkner.

By the late 1880s, Clay had become quite a businessman and had ties to several fabric mills. He came up with a concept for britches called "Gorilla Pants," under the guise that they were so strong not even a gorilla could tear them apart. He had a giant gorilla painted on the side of one of his mills, sporting a pair of Gorilla Pants!

In 1896, an issue of the *Southern Standard* newspaper said, "The Mountain City Woolen Mills is one of the best equipped and best managed manufacturing plants in the state, and its product of Jeans and Gorilla Pants are growing in popular favor and demand."

Clay Faulkner was doing very well with his business, and one of the reasons was that he took such good care of the workers there, providing them affordable homes, a company store with fresh food and supplies, even medical care. His people were loyal to their jobs and to their employer.

When floods threatened his mills, Clay diversified into other businesses and became just as successful there, if not more so. It was during this time that he began work on the home that would be known as Falcon Rest — and later Falcon Manor.

The Victorian mansion was built in 1896, and when it was finished Clay and his wife, Mary, lived there with their five children in true elegance for that period of time. The house had indoor plumbing, electric lights throughout, more than one telephone, and water systems to heat and cool the home. The house is positioned in such a manner that a constant, cool breeze blows over the porches that face north and east. Every element of design and construction was attended to by Faulkner, and the result was a house that became an overnight legend.

Clay Faulkner passed away in the house in 1916, and his wife, Mary, sold the house and moved away. After passing through several owners, in 1929 the house was purchased by Dr. Herman Reynolds, who had a clinic there for both medical and dental practices. It changed hands several more times, often serving as a house but also as a hospital, a sanitarium or two, and a retirement home. It was even owned for a while by the Cumberland Conference of Seventh Day Adventists.

In 1968 it was functioning as a hospital again. Another facility was opened in town, and the beds of the Faulkner Springs

Hospital, as the mansion was known, were all given away. The doors were closed and locked, and the place remained undisturbed for fifteen years. At that time, the current owners purchased the property, and the latest chapter in the house was begun.

Today, it has been restored to its Victorian elegance. Tours are given daily, and it is the scene of many wonderful celebrations. Some of the previous inhabitants must also be happy with its new incarnation, because they continue to make appearances there.

The first appearance of Mr. Faulkner happened in 1919, just three years after his death. While his grandson was playing around the house, Mr. Faulkner gave him a tree branch — an article that can become anything from a riding horse to a knight's sword in a young man's mind. Even as an old man, the grandson remembered his grandfather handing the branch to him.

The mother of one of the current owners lived in Falcon Manor for a while, and during that time she reported the distinct sound of footsteps on the stairway. The steps always paused at her door, which used to be the Faulkners' room. Everyone assumed that it was the spirit of old Clay going back to his room, but too much of a gentleman to intrude on a lady currently staying there.

When the mother passed away, the room was eventually opened up to guests. Interesting things began to be reported almost immediately. Guests' personal items were moved around the room, as if Clay were visiting and rearranging the room to his liking.

He has also been heard during the Christmas season, whistling a carol on the stairway — when no one was upstairs or unaccounted for. It was attributed to Clay Faulkner, the man who marketed Gorilla Pants.

A woman in a high-necked dress has also been spotted in the inn standing in an upstairs window. She is carrying a lantern, looking out across the Tennessee countryside. Although no one is sure who she is, the current belief is that the woman is somehow tied to the hospital days of the house.

The gift shop of the house has many interesting photos that show what may be ghosts at the house, and most of the people who work there have a ghostly story to tell. These spirits aren't restless, though. They seem to be simply dropping in on familiar territory to see how things are in today's world.

Falcon Manor embraces this phenomenon, as witnessed by the "Ghosts of the Manor" program. I regret that I wasn't able to attend it — from all indications it promises to be a very entertaining show. Hopefully the owners will continue to put it on — I think that it will be a major draw.

And who knows, with all the humans impersonating ghosts, it just might turn out that the spirit of Clay Faulkner or the lady in the formal dress will join the cast. Who could resist a celebration of a haunting like that?

Falcon Manor
2645 Faulkner Springs Road
McMinnville, TN 37110
(931) 668-4444
www.falconmanor.com

The Most Haunted Place in the Lone Star State

The Grove — Jefferson, Texas

I CAN'T TELL YOU how many places I've run across in my travels that boast the reputation: "The most haunted place in…" where you can finish the sentence with the appropriate city, state, or region.

Such was the case with The Grove, a house in the historic old river port city of Jefferson, Texas. I'd read about it in newspaper articles, magazines, and several books. In one, of course, it was called "The Most Haunted House in the Most Haunted City in Texas." Quite frankly, I'd heard that so many times about so many places that I simply dismissed the reputation. At that time, The Grove had been opened as a restaurant, but when we went to visit, the owner had closed the doors for good. We drove by, then walked past it again on another trip to Jefferson, and finally became interested enough to start doing a little research on the place.

At that point, something completely unexpected happened: My wife and I fell in love with the old house. Its history called out to us, the ghost stories intrigued us, and the wonderful atmosphere of the city drew us in. When a For Sale sign went up in front of the house, we knew that we were destined to be the next caretakers of The Grove. It took us over a year to decide, but the house was calling to us. We finally signed the papers and became the next in a long line of owners going back to 1861.

After owning the house for three years, probably the most frequent question that we get about The Grove is: Is the place really haunted? Every time I hear that, I just think to myself, "Well, they say that it is the most haunted house in…" but you know the rest.

I'm not sure what people expect when they hear that a place is haunted. In the movie *Poltergeist*, Steven Spielberg wrote a scene where Craig T. Nelson takes a camera crew upstairs to see the supernatural activity in his house. On the way up, the cameraman describes how he once filmed a toy car rolling across the floor at such a slow pace that it was undetectable by the naked eye. Nelson opens the door to his daughter's room, and the cameraman is shocked to see everything in the room flying around in circles, levitating, and moving as if caught in a cosmic whirlwind. I think that's what most people expect when they come to The Grove for a tour.

Things do happen all the time, but usually when it's quiet and no one is looking to have some kind of haunted encounter. Sometimes it's little things. For example, one day after packing up the kitchen for renovation, I was moving boxes from there into the side gallery. It was very routine and mundane: Pick up a box in the kitchen, open the door to the gallery, set the box down, then open the door to go back to the kitchen, and repeat. The door between the two rooms is on an automatic closer, so you have to open it when going either direction. After setting one box down in the gallery, I turned around to open the door but it wouldn't budge — I was locked out. It didn't scare me; in fact, it angered me a little bit. I had to take the long way around back to the kitchen, and the whole way I was saying, "Now why in the world would you do that? What possible reason would you have for locking me out of the kitchen when you know that all I have to do is walk right back around?" No spirit voices answered me, of course, and when I got to the kitchen I found that the door had been dead-bolted from the inside. I think that our spirit friends at The Grove are like that, though — a little mischievous, kind of playful, and seemingly happy that we're taking care of the place.

So what is this place that has such a ghostly reputation? Well, it's a wonderful old home built in 1861 by a couple named Frank and Minerva Stilley. Frank was a cotton broker who traveled up and down the river route between Jefferson and New Orleans buying and selling cotton. Because of his Louisiana roots, Frank interjected a Creole architectural influence to the Greek Revival home, and so The Grove was built in a style that is unique to this part of the country. Thankfully, the owners throughout the years have kept the integrity of the house intact, and it stands today much as it did when it was first built.

There are several spirits that inhabit the old house: an old man with a long, white beard who is the protector of the house; a smiling fellow in a black suit who has been seen walking in the garden through the years; and of course the legendary Lady in White.

She has been seen many times by many different people. When a new home was being built in the neighborhood, people reported seeing a white, glowing form standing beside the eastern side of house as if keeping watch over the new construction on the block, even though there was no one living in The Grove at that time.

In the 1990s, the house was opened as a restaurant. During rehearsal for a dinner theater production there, the lighting technician for the play was standing out on the front porch and saw a lady in an old-fashioned white dress walking down the eastern side of the house. When the tech leaned over the railing to tell the mysterious woman that there was no door on that side of the house, the lady in the white dress turned and stepped up through an outside wall. Inside the house, an actress in the center stairwell saw the lady strolling across the room in front of her and then into the western bedroom. She followed the woman, only to find that the bedroom was empty.

The former owner was dusting a trunk in the stairwell one day when he looked up to see the Lady in White walking casually by. He thought that it was an actual person and not a spirit, until he followed her into the east bedroom to find that she had vanished.

She doesn't always show up visually, though. For a period of time when we first purchased The Grove, she walked through our bedroom. My wife woke up on several occasions in the wee hours of the morning to hear footsteps, as if someone was passing by. She turned on the lamp beside the bed the first few times, but there was no one there. Finally, she became so used to the footsteps that she just turned over and went back to sleep.

Over the last few years that we've owned The Grove, we have both seen the Lady in White walk by several times. There doesn't seem to be any pattern to her appearance — night or day, winter or summer — she's keeping her own spectral schedule. The only thing that seems to be consistent is her path. After exploring the history of the house, it becomes very obvious what is happening. The wall that she walks through used to be the back porch of the house in 1861, so she is stepping up onto the porch, then walking through what used to be the back of the house — probably through a door that was there in those days — and then continues on in a path that she remembers in life.

The final story that I'd like to tell about the Lady in White comes from one of the tours that I was conducting of The Grove.

As a tour home, we have people through every weekend. On one particular Sunday morning, we had a very small group — only a husband and wife, in fact. When we stepped into the room where the Lady in White's path originates, long before I even started talking about her, the wife walked into the room then jumped and yelled. When I asked what was wrong, she was clutching her chest like she was out of breath, and said, "It felt like something just passed right through me!" The Lady in White had passed through the room unseen, but her presence was definitely felt.

Who is this lady? Well, obviously someone who lived here before the 1870 expansion of the house, when the back porch existed.

And the man in the garden — why isn't he ever observed inside the house? Well, the historical records indicate that there was once a dogtrot log cabin where the garden is today, so perhaps he is a visitor from a time when the current house didn't even exist.

But these spirits aren't talking. They merely show up occasionally to check on the place. Even the man with the white beard is a bit elusive, since he only appears when we aren't home. For whatever reason, he feels the need to protect the house from strangers.

After all this time living there, we don't believe that there are spirits who are doomed to haunt the grounds of The Grove or souls that are stuck here on this earthly plane. Instead, we feel that the ghosts are just some of the former owners who look back in on the place from time to time. The former owner of The Grove, Patrick Hopkins, has said that if he gets the opportunity to visit the house after he passes on, you can look for him sitting on the portico just inside the front door. As for my wife and I, we have our own spots picked out. She loves the gardens, but I always tell people that I'll be rocking out on the front gallery long after I'm gone from this physical world. People will talk about how the rocker mysteriously begins to move back and forth, and the smell of fresh coffee permeates the air. It's my favorite place in the house. No matter how beautiful the other side is, I know that I'll want to come back to visit The Grove... the most haunted house in Texas!

The Grove Tour Home
405 Moseley St.
Jefferson, TX 75657
www.thegrove-jefferson.com

But Who the Heck Is Ben Lomond?

Ben Lomond Historic Suite Hotel — Ogden, Utah

WHEN VISITING OGDEN, UTAH, you'll find that the city is in the shadow of Mount Ben Lomond, 9,712 feet high, one of the most famous peaks in the northern Wasatch Range. In fact, it is supposedly the inspiration for Paramount Picture's trademark. It doesn't end there, though. There's also a Ben Lomond Trail up the mountain, a Ben Lomond High School, a Ben Lomond Cemetery, a Ben Lomond Golf Course, the Ben Lomond Heights subdivision, a Ben Lomond Community Pool, and even the Ben Lomond Bowling Lanes. I'm sure that there were other things named after Mr. Lomond that I missed, but I found one of the most interesting ones: the Ben Lomond Historic Suite Hotel. It's worth more than a casual look.

Originally the building was named the Bigelow Hotel. It was built in 1927 in the Italian Renaissance Revival style, something that was extremely rare in Utah, even though in the Roaring Twenties it was very popular around the U.S. The hotel was considered one of the three "Grand Hotels" built in the Beehive

State — one of the others has been demolished and the other is now an office building.

Before the current hotel was constructed, a five-story hotel named The Reed was on the property. It was torn down in 1926 in favor of a new, modernized, high-class hotel. A corporation was formed to build the structure; it consisted of three hundred stockholders and a board of directors that was a "who's who" of local business leaders.

After a year of construction, the Bigelow Hotel opened its doors to rave reviews. There was an Arabian coffee shop reminiscent of a Turkish marketplace, an English room modeled after Bromley Castle in England, a Shakespeare room laden with murals, a Florentine ballroom with Italian touches, and a meeting room with the décor of old Spain. There seemed to be no end to the extravagance of the hotel, and it became one of Ogden's premier showplaces.

It was built to serve; there were three hundred fifty guest rooms, dining space for a thousand people, ballrooms, lounges, restrooms, retail stores, and even a bank located in the building. The basement housed the laundry, kitchen, mechanical plant, and other service offices.

Less than a decade later, a new owner changed the name of the place to the Ben Lomond Hotel, which it has kept through the years. It has changed hands several times, been remodeled over and over, and had many owners, including the prestigious Radisson chain of hotels. It now boasts a much smaller number of rooms, but the space has been divided into plush, luxurious suites. As modern as the hotel is on the inside, on the outside it has become a historical landmark; it is registered on both the State and National Historic Registers.

There are also many hauntings that have been reported at the Ben Lomond over the years. If you're riding the elevator, for example, it may stop at floors for which no one pushed a button, nor is anyone waiting there to get on the elevator. It is as if some unseen person decided to stop there.

Visitors who stay in Room 1102 have reported many strange things, but in a hotel where several rooms have ghostly reputations, it's only one of many active places in the building.

One of the most famous ghosts occupies a room right down the hall — 1106. The spirit who frequents it walks down the hall, head bowed, dressed in black. She will enter the room and just stand there, observing the people sleeping inside. Guests have reported a sudden drop of temperature associated with her presence. She was supposed to meet her son there who was returning from World War II, but he was killed just before he was scheduled to fly back. Her presence seems to be waiting still, waiting for her son to return.

The grand staircase is the sight of another haunting, that of a beautiful young lady in a long, formal gown. She has been seen gracefully ascending the stairs, then walking through the hallways of the hotel. If she is present in the elevator, there is a scent of lilac perfume in the air, and it will sometimes stop on the fifth floor. She has even pushed a housekeeper — who is now the housekeeping manager — out of the bathtub during the daily cleaning. The room that she is most often associated with is 1103.

There seem to be several spirits that walk the hallways of the Ben Lomond Historic Suite Hotel, all attributed to people from Ogden's past. The only thing that I can guarantee, though, is that you're going to love your room once you check in. The service is impeccable, and the accommodations are first rate.

All that said, there's one question I was never able to answer, even with everything that I found emblazoned with Mr. Lomond's moniker... and did I mention the Ben Lomond Car Wash, Ben Lomond Dental Clinic, Ben Lomond Heating and Air Conditioning, Ben Lomond Landscape Maintenance, Ben

Lomond Office Equipment, and the Ben Lomond Animal Clinic. No, the one question that I could never get an answer to is: Who the heck is Ben Lomond? I couldn't find a single person who could tell me. Now that this book is out, I'm sure that someone will solve this mystery for me, but during the process of writing it, that question remained as big a mystery as any of the ghost stories that I found.

Ben Lomond Historic Suite Hotel
2510 Washington Blvd.
Ogden, UT 84401
(801) 627-1900

The Love-Spurned Lady

Emily's Bridge — Stowe, Vermont

STORIES ABOUT haunted bridges scare me. Not because of the ghosts that might be there — no, instead I'm just always afraid that I'm going to run into yet another urban legend. In one of my books I wrote about "Cry Baby Bridge" in DeKalb, Texas. As the story goes you just stop on it at night, roll down your windows, turn off your headlights, kill the engine, and then honk the horn three times. You will then hear the cries of the trio of infants that died when their mother's car careened over the edge into the water.

Guess what? With a little research, not only could I not verify the ghost story at all, but I couldn't even pin down the location of the bridge — I found have a dozen supposed "Cry Baby Bridges."

In another book I covered the "Screaming Bridge of Mosier Valley" — and how do the spirits manifest themselves? Drive onto the bridge at midnight, honk your horn, and then look in the water. You'll see the tombstones of the girls who died there; for some inexplicable reason, the markers are lying flat in the water. Sound ridiculous? Well, I found out that the bridge where teenagers practice this ghostly ritual isn't even the legendary

Screaming Bridge. It was torn down years ago, but the story persists.

There is something about bridge ghost stories, with all of their rituals of cutting off the engine, honking your horn a pre-scribed number of times, and so forth, that are just plain foolish. The people who subscribe to rituals such as these assume that you can summon a ghost at will. In my experience, spirits aren't hanging around to perform for us, so any ghost story that has those kinds of trappings is probably an urban legend or some local fabrication concocted for the entertainment of teenagers after the Friday night football game.

When I was given a tip about someplace called "Emily's Bridge" after a girl who hung herself there, imagine my surprise when I discovered that there were no automobile rituals attached to it. No horn honking, no set times to stop there, just a very intriguing story about an unfortunate tragedy and a girl who may have some unresolved business in this world.

Emily's Bridge, a historic old covered bridge, was originally built in 1844 by John W. Smith. At the time, it was called Gold Brook Bridge, because of the legend that gold had been found in the stream below at some point. Another moniker is the Stowe Hollow Bridge, named after the town of Stowe. It wasn't the first bridge to span Gold Brook on that site — an earlier one was built at the turn of the century. Smith saw the need for a larger, more modern bridge, and he incorporated the use of a Howe truss to give the bridge strength. The bridge is currently one of only four in the state of Vermont that uses this kind of truss.

The bridge is currently in very good condition, probably due to the fact that it was officially adopted in 1969 by the city of Stowe. A resolution was passed that would ensure perpetual care for the historic gem.

But what about Emily, the unofficial namesake of this bridge? Well, this is a story that has been alive in the city of Stowe for over one hundred fifty years. After all this time, the story has mutated into several slightly different tales, but they all have the same basic theme. Here's a very common version of the unfortunate lady's story.

In the mid-1800s, not long after John Smith's covered bridge was constructed over Gold Brook, a local girl informed her parents that she had been seeing a young man in town and that they were planning on getting married. Her folks disapproved of their daughter's plans, however, and let her know in no uncertain terms that she would not be engaging in matrimony with her boyfriend — or anyone else without their approval.

Emily ran away that night. She had made prior arrangements to meet her betrothed at the Gold Brook Bridge, so she hurried through the dark to find comfort in his arms. The covered bridge was empty when she arrived, and Emily patiently waited for her love to arrive. The evening hours ticked into those of the morning, and she was still sitting in solitude.

Her fate soon became evident: Her boyfriend didn't want to marry her, and she'd already stormed out of her parents' house, so if she were to go back she'd have to crawl back in humility. Because her spirit was crushed, Emily found a rope and fashioned a makeshift noose. She tied it to one of the rafters of the covered bridge, then hung herself.

The next morning, the first travelers across the bridge found the terrible sight: Emily's body gently swinging in the early morning breeze.

Soon after she had been buried and the townspeople were starting to put the incident behind them, strange things started to occur on Gold Brook Bridge. As horses and buggies would pass over, some unseen hand would reach out to scratch their sides, like long fingernails were digging into the wood. The world eventually became more modern, and cars replaced the carriages

— but the occasional scratching on their sides continued to be heard.

Other manifestations of Emily have been experienced over the years. The form of a girl has been seen on the bridge by many people over the years, and most of the folks from Stowe believe it to be the spirit of the young girl returning in hopes of finding her fiancé. It became so evident to them through the years, in fact, that Gold Brook Bridge eventually became known as "Emily's Bridge."

People have even reported hearing a girl's voice. The townspeople don't have a doubt that Emily is returning to the bridge where she died for an occasional visit. This is one bridge ghost story that seems to have merit.

I'll tell you something, though. Taking a note from some of those other urban legends that I mentioned might just enhance the experience at Emily's Bridge. If you visit the bridge at night, turn off your car. Get out and walk onto the bridge. There's no need to blow your horn, check your clock, or do any of that other nonsense. Just enjoy the solitude of the night, listen to the creek bubbling below, and you might just find that you're not quite alone.

Emily's Bridge
(Gold Brook Bridge)
Stowe, Vermont

The Woman in the Window

━━ ∘ ● ∘ ● ∘ ━━

Gadsby's Tavern — Alexandria, Virginia

WHILE VISITING our nation's capital, we decided to set aside one day just to explore the city of Alexandria. We got up early, bought our Metro passes, and took the train to the historic town. In retrospect, I'm not sure that one day was quite enough time — there was just so much to do.

After brunch at a charming little café, we spent a while browsing through some of the many unique shops and boutiques, all within a few blocks walking distance. When we got tired we discovered a delightful brewpub where we enjoyed handcrafted beers, and then decided to explore the historical side of town. That search led us to Gadsby's Tavern, a three-story building that had many stories to tell.

It is actually called Gadsby's Tavern Museum, and it houses both a restaurant and a historical period museum. Two buildings side by side make up the complex: a 1785 tavern and a 1792 hotel. Together they're named for John Gadsby, an Englishman who owned and operated them from 1796 to 1808.

In those days, the local tavern was the epicenter of political life in colonial towns. People would meet there to socialize, conduct business, and even hold political meetings. Gadsby's was certainly no different. The list of past patrons of the tavern reads like a who's who in American history: George Washington, Thomas Jefferson, John Adams, James Madison, John Paul Jones, James Monroe and the Marquis de Lafayette. As we paid our entrance fee for the tour and were led into the building by our guide in period costume, it was hard not to be humbled by the great Americans who'd been there before us.

It was a favorite of the Father of our Country, George Washington. Not only did he attend many balls and social events there, but when the French and Indian War began he used the tavern as his headquarters. From there, he gathered two full companies of men for battle. They marched from the tavern to fight at Great Meadows on July 4, 1754 — a battle in which he was defeated. That wouldn't be the last time he took over the tavern as his own. In 1755, when he served on General Braddock's staff, he established headquarters there once again.

The tavern was the center of many events during the birth of our nation. On June 28, 1788, a public gathering was held there to announce the news that Virginia had ratified the new Constitution.

It was also at the tavern that Washington made a farewell address to his friends and neighbors when he was first elected president, before leaving to serve his country in that capacity. Eight years later, Gadsby's tavern was the scene of a reception to honor his service and his return to life as a private citizen.

George and Martha Washington celebrated the president's birthday there on February 22, 1798, and then almost a year later attended a military ball there where he was honored. In November of 1799, Washington gave his final military review from the steps of Gadsby's Tavern and issued the final military order that he would ever give.

Not all of the memorable people associated with Gadsby's were famous, though. In fact, some are anonymous to this day.

The story is told that as the tavern was shutting down one evening during those days, an English Freemason was discovered to be terribly ill. The members of the Masonic Lodge in Alexandria took care of him, nursing him back to health until he was able to travel once again. He would never give his name, but after several years passed by, two thousand five hundred pieces of cut glass arrived from Britain for the local lodge, each emblazoned with the square and compass emblem of the Masons and the initials and number of the Alexandria Lodge. This is not just a legend, however; today one hundred and seventy-five pieces of the glass still exist.

We loved the tour, visiting the ballroom and the bedrooms and all the other places in Gadsby's Tavern — except for one. There was one bedroom that we were not allowed to enter. Still, the tour was one of the most interesting things that we did on the trip. We quickly made reservations for dinner that evening, then walked the short distance to our next scheduled event: the Alexandria ghost walk.

Our guide was dressed in period costume and carried a lantern as he led us through the streets of town sharing his tales. We were both a little surprised — and excited — when he stopped in front of Gadsby's. He began a story of an anonymous guest there that had taken ill, and we assumed that he was going to tell us about the Mason.

Instead, he shared a tale of a different guest, a woman whose spirit is forever tied to the tavern. In 1816, as the story goes, a ship sailed into the port at Alexandria carrying a man and his beautiful wife. The woman was already ill and badly in need of treatment, and since they were obviously well-to-do, the couple was taken to one of the most posh and respectable places in town: Gadsby's Tavern, of course. They rented a room upstairs above the ballroom, and she was given the best medical care that the town had to offer at the time. Despite the efforts of the local doctor and his nurse, the woman died — but not before she extracted an oath from all those attending: Her identity was never to be revealed.

The mysterious woman was buried in St. Paul's Cemetery in Alexandria, and her table-top tombstone was inscribed: *In memory of the female stranger, died October 14, 1816, age 23 years 8 months.* Her husband disappeared suddenly, leaving all the bills from the boarding, medical care, and burial unpaid. The secret of the woman's identity was never revealed, even though those who knew it were left with the unpaid debt of over one thousand dollars. No one knows why they continued to honor her request — and the answer will never be known.

It was not the last time that the woman was seen, however. She sometimes appears in the window of the upstairs room holding a candle, and can even be heard pacing the floors when the tavern is quiet. The ghost of the female stranger has also been spotted in the ballroom and on the stairways, carrying the candle in her hand and wandering easily along.

When we returned to the tavern for dinner, we were treated to many wonderful things: the staff in period costumes, dining by candlelight, and a delicious meal that would rival any establishment in the country. We talked about the woman who died there, and wondered if it was her room that we were not allowed to enter... and if so, why not? Our waiter didn't know for sure, so instead of pressing the issue with the rest of the staff, we simply enjoyed our meal and toasted the old place with a mug of fine spirits. Old George would have been proud.

Gadsby's Tavern Museum
134 North Royal St.
Alexandria, VA 22314
(703) 838-4242
http://www.gadsbystavern.org

A Place of Healing

Rosario Resort — Eastsound, Washington

YOU OCCASIONALLY hear stories about people with a terminal illness who've been given a short time to live but then experience a miraculous recovery that defies explanation. Such is the story of a man named Robert Moran and the palatial home that he built on Orcas Island in the great state of Washington.

Moran was born in 1857 all the way back in New York City, but at the age of eighteen he found himself on the other side of the country, in Seattle. This move was the start of a very prosperous climb for the young man. In six years' time he'd taken a Canadian wife named Melissa Paul, and by 1887 he had already established a reputation as a shipping magnate. Moran entered the local political arena at that time, first as a city councilman, then as the mayor of Seattle.

By 1906, the extreme pressure of his businesses and political office was taking its toll on Robert Moran. He described the situation as "my extreme nervous condition."

He went to his doctor for treatment, and received some very grim news: He had only a short time to live — one year at the most.

Most people would have started digging their own grave, at least figuratively; they'd have given up and simply waited to die. Not Moran, though. At the age of forty-nine he went into retirement and started purchasing land on Orcas Island in the San Juan Islands of the relatively new state of Washington — almost eight thousand acres' worth by the time he was through. The next step was to build a mansion worthy of a man to spend his last days in — and Rosario was born.

It took three years for him to build, but he constructed a home that was considered to be the showplace of the northwest.

In his music room, Moran installed a stained glass window imported from Brussels, Belgium. But one of the most extravagant pieces in the house was a twenty-six rank Aeolian pipe organ that was installed in the music room. Moran paid sixteen thousand dollars for the instrument, and it contained one thousand nine hundred seventy-two pipes. Since Moran didn't have the musical ability to play it, he had it rigged like a player piano, and he would sit on its bench and entertain his guests. They say that none were the wiser for his little charade.

On the grounds of the estate, Moran included a power plant, machine shop, and a figure-eight pond on beautifully landscaped grounds.

The house itself was an architectural marvel. Its foundation was cut into the solid stone, sixteen feet deep. The walls are concrete, and the doors are solid mahogany imported from Honduras. In fact, the doors were so heavy that Moran had to invent a special hinge, one that he called "the butterfly," to support them. He installed windows with plate glass almost an inch thick. To top it off, the roof itself is layered with six tons of copper sheets.

Robert Moran loved his home. He lived at Rosario until the 1930s, when he died at the ripe old age of eighty-six, proving his doctor to be very, very wrong.

I found quite a lot of resources concerning Rosario's haunted reputation, but not a single one points back to Moran. If he is still wandering the halls of his wonderful old mansion, he is doing so very quietly. The source of the ghostly activity at Rosario is attributed to the wife of the next owner of Rosario, Donald Rheem.

As Moran reached the age of eighty, he decided to sell Rosario. Unfortunately, the country was going through the Great Depression, and after six years of trying he could only sell it at the bargain-basement price of fifty thousand dollars to California industrialist Donald Rheem, who owned a galvanizing plant with his brother Richard. Today, the Rheem brothers' business has grown into one of the world's leading manufacturers of central air-conditioning and heating systems. Chances are, if you don't have a Rheem system in your own house, you know someone who does. But I digress.

Donald Rheem's wife, Alice, was one of the most colorful characters to ever inhabit Orcas Island. She was literally the talk of the town. From all reports, she cruised the nearby town of Eastsound, Washington, in bright red clothes. Sometimes it was a dress, other times a pantsuit, and there has been talk of her appearing on the streets of the city riding a Harley-Davidson motorcycle in a red nightgown. How much of that is true, we'll never know. Many sources report her participation in a local card game that regularly took place at the general store, however.

The reason that the occasional haunting at the Rosario is attributed to Alice Rheem is that the specter of a woman in a billowing red dress and high-heeled shoes has appeared to both guests and employees alike. Other phenomena that occur at the hotel include misty shapes in the hallways and phantom footsteps when no one is there. The front desk has also received calls about a particularly noisy couple in a room that is empty, not having been booked on that specific occasion.

The average traveler might never notice these things, but to the people who work there day in and day out, they do occur. My advice is that when you're traveling in Washington, try to book a couple of days at the Rosario Resort. You'll never forget your stay. You can rent a two-person sea kayak and either take a guided tour or strike off on your own exploratory journey. Another favorite activity is whale watching, since three pods of orca whales reside in the nearby waters during the warmer months of the year. During any saltwater excursions, you're likely to see harbor seals, otters, and even bald eagles, our national bird.

Sound adventurous? It is, believe me, but you're not through there. You can also check into the Rosario's world-class spa, where you will be pampered with treatments like massage therapies, yoga, herbal wraps, special skin care treatments, and, of course, saunas and whirlpools — to name but a few things offered.

A visitor can also enjoy the natural beauty of the Rosario estate. If you attempt to do even a fraction of the activities there, you'll quickly discover that a couple of days is not long enough a stay at all. So take your time, enjoy the beautiful atmosphere of the hotel and the pampering of the spa, and keep your eye open for a flash of red. It might just be Mrs. Rheem dashing through on the way to her latest adventure.

Rosario Resort
1400 Rosario Road
Eastsound, WA 98245
(360) 376-2222
www.rosarioresort.com

The Ghost that Convicted Her Husband

West Virginia State Penitentiary — Moundsville, West Virginia

BEFORE RESEARCH-ING THIS chapter for the book, I'd never heard of a ghost actually playing a part in bring-ing a murderer to justice. It happened, though. It's on the books and in the court record — I'm not sure how anyone can explain the event other than supernatural intervention.

The penal institution where the killer was sentenced to serve time is actually the subject of this chapter, but while researching its famous inmates I ran across the story of the murderer who was convicted by the spirit of his victim, and was truly fascinated. We'll get to that, though. First let's take a look at one of the country's most haunted prisons: the West Virginia State Penitentiary in Moundsville.

To fully understand the nature of the hauntings, it is important to look back at the institution itself: its beginnings, its history, the people who lived — and died — there, and its demise.

Construction for Moundsville Prison, as it was originally called, began in 1866. West Virginia had been admitted to the union just three years prior, and the need for a state prison was apparent. The city of Moundsville was selected for the site because it was close to the then-state capital of West Virginia, Wheeling.

Moundsville was originally named for the Indian burial mounds in the area. Grave Creek Mound, which is one of the nation's largest conical burial mounds, is located there. Relics excavated date back to 800 B.C., making this a location with a very long past.

The prison was constructed to exact specifications: The prison yard was a parallelogram that was 682.5 feet in length by 352.5 feet in width. Surrounding the yard was a stone wall that was five feet thick at the bottom and two and a half feet thick at the top. The foundation of the prison wall was five feet below the ground to prevent inmates from tunneling under. The four corners held turrets so that the guards would have a clear view — and a clear shot — at the entire yard. The prison superintendent's house and prison cell buildings were constructed so that their rear wall formed part of the western wall.

Portions of the facility were opened as they were completed over the next ten years, and the Moundsville Prison opened for full operation in 1876; it had two hundred fifty-one male inmates at that time.

Along with common prison areas such as the offices, dining hall, laundry room, and visitor reception, there were some morbidly interesting places as well. The first executions at the prison were by hanging, so a narrow building called the North Wagon Gate has wooden trapdoors on the second floor that were released to allow the condemned man to fall through once the noose was placed around his neck. The public was allowed to view the hangings there until a particularly gruesome execution in 1931 — when the trapdoor was opened, the body fell through with such force that the condemned man was decapitated. After that, the hangings were moved to a more private location known as "the Annex."

The North Hall contained solitary confinement, or "the Hole," which consisted of small rooms where the most dangerous prisoners were held for twenty-two hours a day. "Rat Row" was a section of the prison reserved especially for informants who would be immediately killed if placed in the general inmate population. The newest execution chamber contained "Old Sparky," the state's electric chair. (Is it just me, or is *every* state's electric chair given that nickname?)

Just north of the main entrance was the two-tiered maximum-security corridor. It was one step down from the Hole but still held dangerous prisoners who were threats to the guards or other inmates. Their time outside of the cell was very restricted, and most inhabitants of this area had to even take their meals there.

The prison was used from its initial opening until 1995, when the doors were finally closed — mainly due to a 1986 West Virginia Supreme Court ruling that keeping the prisoners in the small five foot by seven foot cells there was "cruel and unusual punishment."

The history of the West Virginia State Penitentiary is very dark — eighty-five executions were carried out by hanging, including the aforementioned decapitation, and nine men were electrocuted. In 1965, capital punishment was abolished in West Virginia and Old Sparky was unplugged. Like many other "hard time" prisons, some inmates grew so despondent that they took their own lives. There were also the typical killings among rival inmates, and even two violent riots within the walls. The legacy of death there may have left a few unsettled spirits in Moundsville, for many believe the prison to be haunted.

Many visitors have had supernatural encounters there, because when the penitentiary closed, the Moundsville Economic Development Council leased the facility and opened it up for historical and educational tours. You can walk its halls and grounds during the day or take a special nighttime ghost tour.

During a visit, you may hear footsteps pacing the empty corridors that may belong to a prisoner who died there but is still making a nightly walk back to his cell. Another phenomenon are voices calling from the cells, much like it might have been in the dead of night when the place was still occupied by inmates.

One of the most common experiences, however, is more of a feeling. While walking along an empty hallway, you may step into an area where the temperature is noticeably lower; the hair on your arms and the back of your neck will stand up as if you are in an electromagnetic field. An intense emotional feeling often sweeps over people during such an encounter — in such a case, it may be that you are having a personal encounter with one of the former inmates there.

Some of the people who made Moundsville their home were quite famous, including the madman Charles Manson, who led his cult-like "family" to go on a murdering spree in the 1960s.

My favorite story about an inmate there, however, is that of Edward Stribbling Trout Shue. He was a man who might have gotten away with murder, until the spirit of his victim returned to make sure that justice was carried out.

Elva Zona Heaster married Edward Stribbling Trout Shue on October 26, 1896. She was a troubled girl who had already experienced a scandalous out-of-wedlock pregnancy, and he was a blacksmith who was new to the town of Greenbriar, West Virginia. Zona's mother did not approve of the marriage, but the couple professed to be so in love that they went ahead with their matrimonial plans.

Three months later, Edward was in town and sent a young lad back to his home to ask Zona if she wanted him to pick up anything from the store while he was there. The boy entered the house, only to find Zona's lifeless body lying on the floor. He was terrified, and ran for help.

It was about an hour before the city official — a local physician and coroner, Dr. George W. Knapp — arrived at the Shue home. When he did, he found that a hysterical Edward had carried his wife's lifeless body upstairs to their bedroom. He had redressed her in the finest dress that she owned and covered her face with a veil. The doctor tried to examine the body to determine the cause of death, but the wailing and moaning of the widower made it a difficult task. Edward insisted on cradling his wife's head in his arms, so the doctor finally gave up, attributing the death to an "everlasting faint," although the official reason given was "death in childbirth." Before he left, however, the doctor noticed a slight discoloration of Zona's cheek, but with Edward carrying on so, it was simply easier to ignore.

Zona Heaster Shue was laid to rest in the local cemetery, but before the coffin was closed her mother, Mary Jane Heaster, took a sheet from the coffin that had been rolled up beside her daughter's head. It was one of the few keepsakes that Edward had allowed her to take. When she got home, she noticed an odd smell emanating from the cloth, so she decided to wash it. When she put it in a basin of water, a pink color began to ooze from the cloth. She poured some of the water out, but to her surprise, it was clear once removed from the basin. It was a strange experience, but it was only the beginning. Mary Jane unfolded the sheet to find that it now had a pink stain on it — and no matter how she tried to remove it, the fabric would not give up the color.

She felt that this was a sign from her departed daughter, so Mary Jane began to pray every day that if there was some way, her daughter would return to tell her what had happened to cause her death. In a few weeks, the spirit of Zona appeared to her mother over a period of four nights. She told a horrible tale of her marriage, of an abusive husband who beat her viciously and regularly. On the day of her death, she had told Edward that there was no meat in the house to prepare a meal, and he lashed out once again — this time, striking her hard enough to break her neck. With that final revelation, the spirit turned her head completely around.

Mary Jane went immediately to the town prosecutor, John Alfred Preston. Mr. Preston listened to her story, and while he may not have believed it, Mary Jane was so insistent that he felt he should investigate the matter further. There was the issue of the cause of death, which had hardly been deterministic. Several people had also reported that Zona's neck appeared particularly loose when she was being moved into the coffin. The thing that most roused his suspicion, however, was the strange behavior that Edward had exhibited, not letting anyone near the body and insisting that he be the only one to touch her.

Under Mr. Preston's direction, the body was exhumed, and the truth was discovered. Not only did Zona suffer a broken neck, but her windpipe was crushed from strangulation.

Edward was arrested for murder, and during his trial a very violent past was discovered. He had been in trouble with the law before, and had been married twice. The first marriage ended because of his violence toward his wife; his second wife died of a blow to the head under very mysterious circumstances.

Shue was convicted of the murder of his wife and was sentenced to life in prison for his crime. He was taken to the West Virginia State Penitentiary in Moundsville, where he died on March 13, 1900. With all of the supernatural activity at the prison today, it may be that Edward never left.

Moundsville Economic Development Council
818 Jefferson Ave.
Moundsville, WV 26041
(304) 845-6200
www.wvpentours.com

The Sports Fan Spirit

The Pfister Hotel — Milwaukee, Wisconsin

I'VE NEVER SEEN the Sistine Chapel, so I can't use it as a basis for comparison. I hear that it's one of the most beautiful ceilings in the world, though. Gazing up at the ceiling of the three-story lobby in Milwaukee's Pfister Hotel, I have to wonder if it doesn't run a close second. It is a wonderfully detailed skyscape, with rolling clouds and cherubs playing among them. Trust me, it's one of those things where you walk in, look up, and just say, "Wow."

It's not just the ceiling, though. The hotel lobby is extravagant with its heavy square columns and gilded trim, and rivals any that I traveled to in the course of writing this book.

By now you probably know how fascinating I find history, and so examining the Pfister was quite an experience. When you look at the Romanesque Revival building from the outside, the first thing that you notice is that the bottom three floors are limestone and the upper five floors are built with Milwaukee's cream-colored brick — or Cream City Brick as it is known — with terra cotta trim.

The hotel was the vision of a man named Guido Pfister, a German immigrant and tanner who rose to prominence in Milwaukee during the 1840s, and established himself as a community leader. He spent much of his life planning the hotel, looking at it as a grand salon for the city where visitors from all over the world would be welcome. Construction was slated to begin in 1890, but unfortunately, Guido passed away in 1889. His son Charles took the reins and began to make his father's dream come true.

By 1893, and after an unheard-of cost of over one million dollars, the hotel was complete and opened its doors. On May 2, 1893, the *Milwaukee Sentinel* newspaper said that the Pfister's grand opening was "in a way to Milwaukee what the opening of the World's Fair was to Chicago." The hotel redefined extravagance with full electrical wiring throughout the building and its own generators to provide the power, climate controls in each room, and fire protection second to no other place in the country.

Visitors there could find every amenity: a soda fountain, a druggist, a barbershop, and even lounges segregated between men and women. The gentlemen were allowed to go into the ladies' lounge, but women were forbidden in the men's lounge.

A few years after it opened, the Pfister played host to U.S. President William McKinley and his Cabinet. Since then, it has welcomed many other presidents, not to mention dignitaries from other countries, royalty, prime ministers, and stars of stage, screen, and the sports world.

By 1962, like any grand old lady, the hotel was starting to show her age. The Pfister was purchased by a businessman named Ben Marcus, who wanted to restore the hotel to its original beauty. Some will turn up their nose at his changes, which included the twenty-three story circular wing and the parking garage. It may seem a bit garish in comparison to the original hotel, but in today's world I believe that it adds an interesting, retro '60s look. Whatever one might think, Marcus' additions have become a part of the history of the Pfister.

A walk around the inside of the Pfister is not unlike a visit to a fine museum. Stop by the concierge desk, and you can pick up a brochure cataloging the hotel's artwork. From what I hear, the Victorian paintings from Guido and Charles Pfister's collection make up the world's largest collection of Victorian art on permanent display in a hotel. It represents German, Italian, French, and American artists. In the lobby, in the hallways, on the walls of the restaurants, and up on the mezzanine level, you will find over eighty spectacularly framed watercolor and oil paintings from the nineteenth and early twentieth centuries.

As I rave on about this beautiful hotel, though, you must have determined by now that it has a ghost story or two that are begging to be told — and you are correct. The most common occurrence is the sighting of what hotel employees describe as a well-dressed gentleman, an older, portly fellow who has been spotted in the hallways and on the grounds. Employees see him, then glance back to find that he has completely disappeared. Many think that this is the spirit of Charles Pfister, builder of the hotel, who is simply returning to make sure that his namesake is still running efficiently and catering to the needs of all the guests.

Now, I can't say for sure that the spirits of the hotel are sports fans, but they did pay special attention to a particular baseball player one evening. The hotel is often used by professional baseball players in town to face the Brewers, and according to the August 20, 2001, issue of *Sports Illustrated* magazine, L.A. Dodger third baseman Andre Beltre had a haunted encounter there. The team checked in late on the evening of July 23, when the hotel was still and quiet. Beltre said that even though the hallway outside his room was empty, as he was going to bed he heard knocking outside and on his door. Inside the room, the television and air conditioner kept turning on and off by themselves.

Rapping noises then began to issue from his headboard, allowing him only a few hours' sleep for the evening.

Many people on staff have their own ghost stories to share, and it is a lot of fun to spend some time just talking to them. One thing is certain — you will feel like a dignitary during your stay at the Pfister. The turndown service leaves not only a chocolate on your pillow, but the weather forecast as well. You will also find a Sweet Dreams prayer placed there for you: "Because this hotel is a human institution to serve people, and not solely a money-making organization, we hope that God will grant you peace and rest while you are under our roof. May the business that brought you our way prosper. May every call you make and every message you receive add to your joy... may this room and hotel be your 'second home.' "

You will love the Pfister, and it may be that Charles himself pays you a visit just to make sure that you do. If you want to treat yourself to a truly extravagant experience while you're there, just go up to the twenty-third floor to Blu, the hotel's famous lounge. Take a seat in one of the plush couches or wingback chairs, and sip on one of Blu's various signature martinis while you look out of the picture windows at downtown Milwaukee or Lake Michigan. Ahhhh, I'm relaxed just thinking about it. Charles would be proud.

The Pfister Hotel
424 East Wisconsin Ave.
Milwaukee, WI 53202
(414) 390-3832
www.thepfisterhotel.com

The Female Spirit in Our Room

The Irma Hotel — Cody, Wyoming

WYOMING IS A territory that everyone should find time to visit — it's like going back and looking at a page of America's past. From the Badlands region with sunsets that will take your breath away to the subtle majesty of the Big Horn Mountains, you'll be amazed by the beauty of the countryside. When looking across the countryside, it's downright impossible to keep from imagining how it must feel to have been traveling across the country in a covered wagon, braving the new frontier, and seeing the countryside of Wyoming for the first time.

Of course, when talking about Wyoming, one has to mention the mysterious Devil's Tower, a circular monolith that rises over twelve hundred feet above the surface. I'm sure that most everyone will recognize it from the movie *Close Encounters of the Third Kind* — it's the place where the alien ship set down to make contact.

Devil's Tower is sacred to several American Indian tribes, who know the place as "waken," which means a sacred place. At least six tribes — the Arapahoe, Cheyenne, Lakota, Crow, Kiowa, and Shoshone — attach a special reverence to the Devil's Tower.

There are several legends as to how the tower was created, but one of the most interesting comes from the Kiowa. In their story, seven Kiowa girls were out exploring the countryside around their home. They wandered a bit too far, however, and ventured into an area where wild animals roamed. A group of bears noticed the children and, thinking that they would be a wonderful snack, began to chase them. The girls sought refuge on top of a huge rock, but it was not tall enough to protect them from the beasts. The Great Spirit looked down favorably upon the children, though, and caused the rock to rise up out of the ground toward the heavens. The bears surrounded the rock and began to claw at its sides in an attempt to climb up to get the girls. The animals did not succeed, of course, but you can still see their massive claw marks on the sides of the rock. The girls never met their terrible fate with the bears. Instead, each was taken up to the heavens and became a shining star.

The seven stars are still in the sky today — the Pleiades star cluster. Because of this legend, to the Lakota the place is known as "Bear's Lodge," the Arapaho call it "Bear's Tipi," and it has a similar name among many tribes.

While planning our trip to Wyoming, we found many other fascinating places such as Yellowstone and the Grand Tetons. We spent a little extra time surfing the 'Net for interesting things to do in the state and found a mention about a Wyoming hotel that Buffalo Bill Cody built. It was located in the town that bears his name, and the web page further went on to say that the historic Irma Hotel in Cody, Wyoming, had more than its share of spirits.

The place was built by Buffalo Bill in 1902, and was named for his daughter Irma. He retained two suites and an office there for his personal use, and in fact, would conduct auditions for his Wild

West Show out on the porch that wraps around the front of the hotel.

Because of the history of the hotel and the town of Cody, and of course the reported haunting there, we detoured a little off course during our Yellowstone vacation to spend an evening at the Irma.

We arrived at the place that Buffalo Bill called "just the sweetest hotel that ever was," and immediately located the dining room for a bit of lunch. We noticed a huge bar along one wall, and when a waitress saw us admiring it she said that it was very famous, since it dated back to the period when the hotel was first built. It is made of cherrywood, and with its intricate carving and embedded cases and mirrors, the piece is one of the most photographed items in the hotel.

The food was good, the service was very attentive, and once we got our bellies full after the drive from Yellowstone, it was time to retire to our room.

We had booked the Colonel Cody suite, which had belonged to old Buffalo Bill himself, and as soon as I opened the door, my wife took a step in and said, "I can't stay here. Something doesn't want me in this room."

After such a long drive, I wasn't about to go hunting another place so I dismissed her hesitation with a wave of my hand. "There's nothing in here to worry about," I told her, and we went on to explore the suite.

It was simple yet elegant, and we could imagine Mr. Cody himself walking across the suite and out onto the balcony. Something was still bothering my wife, but I kept insisting that it was only her imagination. That's when the weird stuff started happening.

Now, I try to come down on the skeptical side of things, and I was doing my best to explain away everything that was happening: The sink faucet turned on by itself, but maybe there was a problem with their plumbing; a door slammed shut in my wife's face, but perhaps there was a draft in the room; you get the idea.

With every little thing that happened, she felt more and more unwelcome. Finally, she said, "I can't tell you why, but I believe that there's a female presence here that isn't happy about me being in the room."

Deny it as I tried, the host of little things that were happening to her in the room increased, and it was getting harder to convince her to stay. The culmination of the evening came when we were sitting out on the balcony watching a gorgeous sunset. We'd stopped at a local store and purchased two plastic wineglasses and a bottle of Chardonnay, and were sipping our drinks and talking about the vacation. I was directly facing her, and as we were speaking, the glass of wine was slapped out of her hand by some unseen force — the plastic wineglass went skipping across the balcony.

Keep in mind that I was staring *directly at her.* She didn't drop the glass, she didn't toss it; she was merely holding it when something knocked it away.

"That's it. I'm outta here!" she said, standing up to leave the hotel.

I was still a little shocked. We visit haunted placcs across the country, but we don't often have an experience in the one or two evenings that we're there — certainly not of this magnitude!

I didn't want to leave, though, because it was getting late and our other prospects in town wouldn't be anything like the room that we'd booked at the Irma.

So I took a chance.

I asked my wife to just wait a few minutes and let me try something a little radical. I went back into the room and began speaking to whatever presence might be there. I said something to the effect of, "To whatever spirit might be in this room — my wife and I are staying here for the evening, but we're only guests.

We'll be leaving in the morning, and we certainly don't mean any disrespect or harm. You've been bothering my wife since we've come in, making her feel unwelcome, and I would like to kindly ask you to stop. Let us spend the night, and we'll be gone. We certainly don't want to make you mad; we're simply enjoying the beauty of the hotel and the warmth of your room."

I went back out onto the balcony and told my wife what I'd done, and with a little apprehension, she walked back into the room. "This is completely different," she said with a smile. "For the first time, I feel like it's okay for me to be here."

From that point on, we had a wonderful time at the Irma. We had drinks in the bar and visited with one of the waitresses who told us ghost story after ghost story: a figure who's been seen on the stairs that many believe to be Buffalo Bill; a knocking on the wall of the hallway beside the room that we were staying in; and many other tales that we were fascinated by. In our eyes, they all paled in comparison to the experience that we'd had upstairs.

We also walked around the hotel and couldn't help but think that we were walking in the footsteps of that Wild West hero, who in 1902 told the Lincoln, Nebraska, *Trade Review,* "As long as we are bound to have a hotel, let's have a dandy. I am going to spare no expense in furnishing it. It must be a gem... I am going to run this hotel myself if I have to keep the Wild West Show running winter and summer to keep it going."

The Irma is listed on the National Register of Historic Places by the National Park Service, and believe me, it just oozes history. The staff is friendly, and once we had a talk with the ghost that was bothering my wife, our stay was delightful.

While you're in Cody, don't miss the Buffalo Bill Historical Center or the gunfight reenactment in the street beside the hotel. There are also a number of shops to browse through, and we spent so much time there that we ended up having some items shipped back home. Most of all though, we enjoyed our evening at the Irma. We sat on the balcony, sipping wine and watching the sun go down. It was romantic, it was magical, and our earlier experience there gave us a story that we'll be telling for a lifetime.

The Irma Hotel
1192 Sheridan Ave.
Cody, WY 82414
(307) 587-4221
(800) 745-IRMA
www.irmahotel.com

A Few Words in Closing

Wow — what a journey. Have we really been to all fifty states? I don't know when I've had as much fun, and I hope that you enjoyed it as well. I wouldn't mind going back and starting it all over again!

All of the places that we visited are open to the public in one fashion or another, so I encourage you to make your own journey to visit them.

I wrote the first words of this book sitting in a room at the Crescent Hotel in Eureka Springs, Arkansas, and finished it in a rocking chair at The Grove in Jefferson, Texas. In between, I put a few miles on the car and earned a few frequent flyer points with the airlines. I also made a lot of friends along the way, making the book well worth the effort.

For both of us it's a beginning, however. We have more travels to take, more places to explore, and more ghost stories to chase.

I'm sure that there are a few more spirits lurking over in the Winchester House that we didn't run across, and I'm ready for another order of bangers at the Red Lion Pub.

I really would like to encounter the ghost of Doc Holliday at the Bird Cage Theatre dealing a round of faro, but I'd be happy to simply have another Prosperity Sandwich with the spirits of Lemp Mansin in St. Lewis.

Yes, there are many places to revisit and explore just a little more. And of course, we have plenty of time. Just come with me — I have a road map, a little gas in the tank, and, above all, a ghost in my suitcase!

Look for these titles in the *Haunted Encounters* series:

Haunted Encounters: Real-Life Stories of Supernatural Experiences

ISBN 0-9740394-0-3

Haunted Encounters: Ghost Stories from Around the World

ISBN 0-9740394-1-1

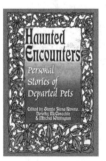

Haunted Encounters: Personal Stories of Departed Pets

ISBN 0-9740394-2-X

Release May 2005

Haunted Encounters: Living in a Haunted House

ISBN 0-9740394-6-2

Haunted Encounters: Departed Family and Friends

ISBN 0-9740394-3-8

Other Books by Atriad Press

Fear: A Ghost Hunter's Story
by Kriss Stephens

ISBN 0-9740394-4-6

Staci's Guide to Animal Movies
by Staci Layne Wilson

ISBN 0-9740394-8-9

Shadows Dancing
True Tales of Shadow People

by Joan and Steve Nuebauer

ISBN 0-9740394-7-0

Available June 2005

For ordering information

www.atriadpress.com

Atriad Press LLC
13820 Methuen Green
Dallas, TX 75240
972-671-0002